ITALIAN

VISUAL
PHRASE BOOK

Previously published as
Italian Visual Phrase Book & CD

LONDON, NEW YORK, MELBOURNE, MUNICH, DELHI

Senior Editor Angela Wilkes
Art Editor Silke Spingies
Production Editor Phil Sergeant
Production Controller Inderjit Bhullar
Managing Editor Julie Oughton
Managing Art Editor Louise Dick
US Editor Margaret Parrish

Produced for Dorling Kindersley by
SP Creative Design

Language content by First Edition
Translations Ltd, Cambridge, UK
Translator Esmeralda Lines
Editor Gabriella Barra
Typesetting Essential Typesetting

First American Edition, 2009
Published in the United States by
DK Publishing, 375 Hudson Street, New
York, New York 10014

12 13 14 15 16 10 9 8 7 6 5 4 3 2
001–183055–July/2012

Published in Great Britain by
Dorling Kindersley Limited

A catalog record for this book is available
from the Library of Congress
ISBN 978-0-7566-9240-7

Previously published as
Italian Visual Phrase Book & CD
ISBN 978-0-7566-3684-5

DK books are available at special discounts
when purchased in bulk for sales
promotions, premiums, fund-raising, or
educational use. For details, contact DK
Publishing Special Markets, 375 Hudson
Street, New York, New York, 10014 or
SpecialSales@dk.com

Printed and bound in China by Leo Paper
Products LTD

Discover more at
www.dk.com

CONTENTS

INTRODUCTION

This book provides all the key words and phrases you are likely to need in everyday situations. It is grouped into themes, and key phrases are broken down into short sections, to help you build a wide variety of sentences. A lot of the vocabulary is illustrated to make it easy to remember, and "You may hear" boxes feature questions you are likely to hear. At the back of the book there is a menu guide, listing about 500 food terms, and a 2,000-word two-way dictionary. Numbers and the most useful phrases are listed on the jacket flaps for quick reference.

Nouns

All Italian nouns (words for things, people, and ideas) are masculine or feminine. The gender of singular nouns is usually shown by the word for "the": **il** or **lo** (masculine) and **la** (feminine). They change to **l'** before vowels. The plural forms are **i** or **gli** (masculine) and **le** (feminine).

Adjectives

Most Italian adjectives change endings according to whether they describe a masculine or feminine, singular or plural word. In this book the singular masculine form is shown, followed by the alternative feminine ending:

I'm lost   **Mi sono perso/a**

"You"

There are two ways of saying "you" in Italian: **lei** (polite) and **tu** (familiar). In this book we have used **lei** throughout, as that is what you normally use with people you don't know.

Verbs

Verbs change according to whether they are in the singular or plural. In phrases where this happens, the singular form of the verb is followed by the plural form:

Where is/are…?   **Dov'è/Dove sono…?**

Pronunciation guide

Below each Italian word or phrase in this book, you will find a pronunciation guide in italics. Read it as if it were English and you should be understood, but remember that it is only a guide and for the best results you should listen to and mimic native speakers. Some Italian sounds are different from those in English, so take note of how the letters below are pronounced.

a	like a in car
ai	like i in mile
ao, au	like ow in cow
c	before a, o, and u, like k in kite
	before i and e, like ch in church
cc	like ch in church
ch	like k in keep
e	like e in pet
ei	like ay in day
g	before a, o, and u, like g in get
	before i and e, like j in jam
gh	like g in got
gli	like lli in million
gn	like ni in onion
h	silent
i	like ee in keep
o	like o in pot
oi	like oy in boy
qu	like qu in quick
r	rolled
s	like s in see or z in zoo
sc	before a, o, and u, like sk in skip
	before i or e, like sh in ship
u	like oo in boot
z	like ts in pets, or ds in loads

ESSENTIALS

In this section, you will find the essential words and useful phrases you need for basic everyday talk and situations. Be aware of cultural differences when you're addressing Italian people, and also remember that they tend to be somewhat formal when they are greeting each other, using *signore* (for men), *signora* (for women), and *signorina* (for girls and younger women). These titles are also used with last names.

GREETINGS

Hello	Salve *salveh*
Good evening	Buonasera *bwonaserah*
Good night	Buonanotte *bwonanotteh*
Goodbye	Arrivederci *arreevederchee*
Hi/bye!	Ciao/ciao! *chow*
Pleased to meet you	Piacere *pyachereh*
How are you?	Come sta? *komeh stah*
Fine, thanks	Bene, grazie *beneh gratsye*
You're welcome	Prego *pregoh*
My name is…	Mi chiamo… *mee kyamoh*
What's your name?	Come si chiama? *komeh see kyamah*
What's his/her name?	Lui/lei come si chiama? *looee/lay komeh see kyamah*
This is…	Questo/a è… *kwestoh/ah eh*
Nice to meet you	Lieto/a di conoscerla *lyetoh/ah dee konosherlah*
See you tomorrow	A domani *ah domanee*
See you soon	A presto *ah prestoh*

SMALL TALK

Yes/no	Sì/no *see/noh*
Please	Per favore *pehr favoreh*
Thank you (very much)	(Molte) grazie *(molteh) gratsye*
You're welcome	Prego *pregoh*
OK/fine	OK/bene *okay/beneh*
Pardon?	Scusi? *skoozee*
Excuse me	Mi scusi *mee skoozee*
Sorry	Mi dispiace *mee deespyacheh*
I don't know	Non so *non soh*
I don't understand	Non capisco *non kapeeskoh*
Could you repeat that?	Può ripetere? *pwo reepetereh*
I don't speak Italian	Non parlo italiano *non parloh eetalyanoh*
Do you speak English?	Parla inglese? *parlah eengleseh*
What is the Italian for…?	Come si dice in italiano…? *komeh see deeche een eetalyanoh*
What's that?	Cos'è quello/a? *kozeh kwelloh/ah*
What's that called?	Come si chiama? *komeh see kyamah*
Can you tell me…	Mi può dire… *mee pwoh deereh*

TALKING ABOUT YOURSELF

I'm from…	Vengo da… *vengoh dah*
I'm…	Sono… *sonoh*
…English	…inglese *eengleseh*
…American	…americano/a *amereekanoh/ah*
…Canadian	…canadese *kanadezeh*
…Australian	…australiano/a *owstralyanoh/ah*
…single	…celibe/nubile *cheleebeh/noobeeleh*
…married	…sposato/a *sposatoh/ah*
…divorced	…divorziato/a *deevortsyatoh/ah*
I am…years old	Ho…anni *oh…annee*
I have…	Ho… *oh*
…a boyfriend	…un fidanzato *oon feedantsatoh*
…a girlfriend	…una fidanzata *oonah feedantsatah*

You may hear…

- **Da dove viene?**
  dah doveh vyeneh
  Where are you from?

- **È sposato/a?**
  eh sposatoh/ah
  Are you married?

- **Ha figli?**
  ah feelye
  Do you have children?

SOCIALIZING

Do you live here?	Vive qui? *veeveh kwee*
Where do you live?	Dove vive? *doveh veeveh*
I am here...	Sono qui... *sonoh kwee*
...on vacation	...in vacanza *een vakantsah*
...on business	...per lavoro *pehr lavoroh*
I'm a student	Sono uno/a studente/ studentessa *sonoh oonoh/ah stoodente/stoodentessah*
I work in...	Lavoro a... *lavoroh ah*
I am retired	Sono pensionato/a *sonoh penzyonatoh/ah*
Can I have...	Posso avere... *possoh avereh*
...your telephone number?	...il suo numero di telefono? *eel soowoh noomeroh dee telefonoh*
...your email address?	...il suo indirizzo e-mail? *eel soowoh eendeereedzo emayl*
It doesn't matter	Non importa *non eemportah*
Cheers	Cin cin *cheen cheen*
Do you mind if I smoke?	Le dispiace se fumo? *leh deespyache seh foomoh*
I don't drink/smoke	Non bevo/fumo *non bevoh/foomoh*
Are you alright?	Sta bene? *stah beneh*

LIKES AND DISLIKES

I like/love...	Mi piace/adoro... *mee pyacheh/adoroh*
I don't like...	Non mi piace... *non mee pyacheh*
I hate...	Detesto... *detestoh*
I really like...	Mi piace abbastanza/ molto... *mee pyacheh abbastantsa/ moltoh*
Don't you like it?	Non le piace? *non leh pyacheh*
I would like...	Vorrei... *vorray*
My favorite is...	Il mio preferito è... *eel meeoh prefereetoh eh*
I prefer...	Preferisco... *prefereeskoh*
I think it's great	Penso che sia fantastico *penzoh keh sya fantasteeko*
It's delicious	È delizioso/a *eh deleetsyosoh/ah*
What would you like to do?	Cosa vorrebbe fare? *kozah vorrebbeh fareh*
I don't mind	Non mi dispiace *non mee deespyacheh*

You may hear...

- Di cosa si occupa?
dee kozah see okoopah
What do you do?

- È in vacanza?
eh een vakantsah
Are you on vacation?

- Le piace...?
leh pyacheh
Do you like...?

DAYS OF THE WEEK

What day is it today?	Che giorno è oggi? *keh jornoh eh ojee*
Sunday	domenica *domeneekah*
Monday	lunedì *loonedee*
Tuesday	martedì *martedee*
Wednesday	mercoledì *merkoledee*
Thursday	giovedì *jovedee*
Friday	venerdì *venerdee*
Saturday	sabato *sabatoh*
today	oggi *ojee*
tomorrow	domani *domanee*
yesterday	ieri *yeree*
in…days	tra…giorni *trah…jornee*

THE SEASONS

primavera
preemaverah
spring

estate
estateh
summer

MONTHS

January	gennaio *jenayo*
February	febbraio *febrayo*
March	marzo *martso*
April	aprile *apreeleh*
May	maggio *majjo*
June	giugno *joonyo*
July	luglio *loolyo*
August	agosto *agostoh*
September	settembre *setembreh*
October	ottobre *otobreh*
November	novembre *novembreh*
December	dicembre *deechembreh*

autunno
owtoonnoh
fall

inverno
eenvernoh
winter

TELLING THE TIME

What time is it?	Che ore sono? *keh oreh sonoh*
It's nine o'clock	Sono le nove *sonoh leh noveh*
...in the morning	...del mattino *del matteenoh*
...in the afternoon	...del pomeriggio *del pomereedjoh*
...in the evening	...della sera *dellah serah*

l'una
loonah
one o'clock

l'una e dieci
loonah eh deeaychee
ten past one

l'una e un quarto
loonah eh oon kwartoh
quarter past one

l'una e venti
loonah eh ventee
twenty past one

l'una e mezza
loonah eh medza
half past one

due meno un quarto
dooeh menoh oon kwartoh
quarter to two

due meno dieci
dooeh menoh deeaychee
ten to two

le due
leh dooeh
two o'clock

It's noon/midnight	È mezzogiorno/mezzanotte *eh medzojornoh/ medzanotteh*
second	il secondo *eel sekondoh*
minute	il minuto *eel meenootoh*
hour	l'ora *lorah*
a quarter of an hour	un quarto d'ora *oon kwartoh dorah*
half an hour	mezz'ora *medzorah*
three-quarters of an hour	tre quarti d'ora *tray kwartee dorah*
late	tardi *tardee*
early/soon	presto/presto *prestoh*
What time does it start?	A che ora inizia? *ah keh orah eeneetsya*
What time does it finish?	A che ora finisce? *ah keh orah feeneesheh*
How long will it last?	Quanto tempo durerà? *kwantoh tempoh doorerah*

You may hear...

- **A presto.**
  ah prestoh
  See you later.

- **È in anticipo.**
  eh een anteecheepoh
  You're early.

- **È in ritardo.**
  eh een reetardoh
  You're late.

THE WEATHER

What's the forecast?	Quali sono le previsioni? *kwalee sonoh leh preveesyonee*
What's the weather like?	Che tempo fa? *ke tempoh fah*
It's...	È... *eh*
...good	...buono *bwonoh*
...bad	...cattivo *kateevoh*
...warm	...mite *meeteh*
...hot	...caldo *kaldoh*
...cold	...freddo *freddoh*

È soleggiato
eh solejatoh
It's sunny

È piovoso
eh pyovozoh
It's raining

È nuvoloso
eh noovolozoh
It's cloudy

È tempestoso
eh tempestozoh
It's stormy

What's the temperature?	Qual è la temperatura? *kwaleh lah temperatoorah*
It's…degrees	Ci sono…gradi *chee sonoh…gradee*
It's a beautiful day	È una bellissima giornata *eh oonah beleesseemah jornatah*
The weather's changing	Il tempo sta cambiando *eel tempoh stah kambyandoh*
Is it going to get colder/ hotter?	Farà più freddo/caldo? *farah pew freddoh/kaldoh*
It's getting cooler	La temperatura sta scendendo *lah temperatoorah stah shendendoh*

Nevica
neveeka
It's snowing

È ghiacciato
eh gyatchyatoh
It's icy

C'è nebbia
che nebbyah
It's misty

È ventoso
eh ventozoh
It's windy

GETTING AROUND

Italy has an excellent road and highway system
if you are traveling around the country by car,
although you have to pay a toll (*un pedaggio*) to
use the fast highways (*autostrade*). Italian trains,
linking the main towns and cities, are fast, punctual,
and surprisingly inexpensive. In large cities you can
get around by taxi, bus, or tram. In Milan there is
also the subway (*metropolitana*).

ASKING WHERE THINGS ARE

Excuse me	Mi scusi *mee skoozee*
Where is...	Dov'è... *doveh*
...the town center?	...il centro della città? *eel chentroh dellah cheetah*
...the railroad station?	...la stazione ferroviaria? *lah statsyoneh ferovyarya*
...a cash machine?	...uno sportello bancomat? *oonoh sportelloh bankomat*
How do I get to...?	Come posso arrivare a...? *komeh possoh arreevareh ah*
I'm going to...	Sto andando a... *stoh andandoh ah*
I'm looking for...	Sto cercando... *stoh cherkandoh*
I'm lost	Mi sono perso/a *mee sonoh persoh/ah*
Is it near?	Si trova qui vicino? *see trovah kwee veecheenoh*
Is there a...nearby?	C'è un...qui vicino? *che oon...kwee veecheenoh*
Is it far?	È lontano? *eh lontanoh*
How far is...	Quanto dista... *kwantoh deestah*
...the town hall?	...il municipio? *eel mooneecheepyo*
...the market?	...il mercato? *eel merkatoh*
Can I walk there?	Posso arrivarci a piedi? *possoh arreevarchee ah pyedee*

CAR RENTAL

Where is the car rental desk?	Dov'è l'ufficio dell'autonoleggio? *doveh loofeechyo del owtonoledjoh*
I want to rent...	Vorrei noleggiare... *vorray noledjareh*
...a car	...un'automobile *oon owtomobeeleh*
...a bicycle	...una bicicletta *oonah beecheeklettah*

la berlina
lah berleenah
sedan

il portellone posteriore
eel portelloneh posteryoreh
hatchback

il motociclo
eel motocheekloh
motorcycle

lo scooter
loh scooter
scooter

la mountain bike
lah mountain bike
mountain bike

la bicicletta da strada
lah beecheeklettah dah stradah
road bike

for...days	per...giorni *pehr...jornee*
for a week	per una settimana *pehr oonah setteemanah*

for the weekend	per un fine settimana *pehr oon feeneh setteemanah*
I'd like...	Vorrei... *vorray*
...an automatic	...un'automobile con il cambio automatico *oon owtomobeeleh kon eel kambyo owtomateekoh*
...a stick shift	...un'automobile con il cambio manuale *oon owtomobeeleh kon eel kambyo manwaleh*
Here's my driver's license	Ecco la mia patente di guida *ekko lah mee-ah patenteh dee gweedah*
Can I rent a...	Posso noleggiare... *possoh noledjareh*
Do you have a...	Avete... *aveteh*

il seggiolino per bambini
eel sedjoleenoh pehr bambeenee
child seat

il lucchetto
eel lookettoh
lock

il casco
eel kaskoh
cycling helmet

DRIVING

Is this the road to...?	È questa la strada per...? *eh kwestah lah stradah pehr*
Where is the nearest garage?	Qual è l'officina più vicina? *kwaleh lofeecheenah pew veecheenah*
I'd like...	Vorrei... *vorray*
...some gasoline	...del carburante *del karbooranteh*
...40 liters of unleaded	...quaranta litri di benzina senza piombo *kwarantah leetree dee bentseenah sentsah pyomboh*
...30 liters of diesel	...trenta litri di gasolio *trentah leetree dee gazolyo*
Fill it up, please	Il pieno, per favore *eel pyenoh, pehr favoreh*
Where do I pay?	Dove pago? *doveh pagoh?*
The pump number is...	La pompa numero... *lah pompah noomeroh...*
Can I pay by credit card?	Posso pagare con la carta di credito? *possoh pagareh kon lah kartah dee kredeetoh?*

la stazione di servizio
lah statsyoneh dee serveetsyo
gas station

Can you check...	Può controllare... *pwo kontrollareh*
...the oil	...l'olio *lolyo*
...the tire pressure	...la pressione dei pneumatici *lah pressyoneh day pneuhmateechee*

PARKING

Is there a parking lot nearby?	C'è un parcheggio nelle vicinanze? *che oon parkedjo nelleh veecheenantse*
Can I park here?	Posso parcheggiare qui? *possoh parkedjareh kwee*
Is it free?	È gratuito? *eh gratweetoh*
How much does it cost?	Quanto costa? *kwantoh kostah*
How much is it...	Quanto costa... *kwantoh kostah*
...per hour?	...all'ora? *alorah*
...per day?	...al giorno? *al jornoh*
...overnight?	...fino al giorno dopo? *feenoh al jornoh dopoh*

il portapacchi
eel portapakee
roof rack

il seggiolino per bambini
eel sedjoleenoh pehr bambeenee
child seat

THE CAR

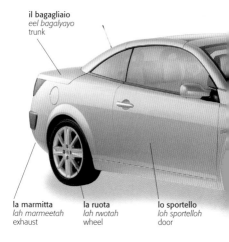

il bagagliaio
eel bagalyayo
trunk

la marmitta
lah marmeetah
exhaust

la ruota
lah rwotah
wheel

lo sportello
loh sportelloh
door

INSIDE THE CAR

il poggiatesta
eel podjatestah
head rest

la maniglia
lah maneelya
handle

la chiusura
lah kewsoorah
door lock

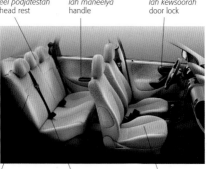

il sedile posteriore
eel sedeeleh posteryoreh
back seat

la cintura di sicurezza
lah cheentoorah dee seekooredza
seat belt

il sedile anteriore
eel sedeeleh anteryoreh
front seat

il parabrezza
eel parabredza
windshield

il cofano
eel kofanoh
hood

i fari
ee faree
headlights

il pneumatico
eel pneoomateekoh
tire

il motore
eel motoreh
engine

il paraurti
eel parowrtee
bumper

THE CONTROLS

l'airbag
lairbag
airbag

le frecce lampeggianti
leh fretcheh lampedjantee
hazard lights

il cruscotto
eel krooskottoh
dashboard

lo sterzo
loh stertso
steering wheel

il tachimetro
eel takeemetroh
speedometer

il clacson
eel klakson
horn

la leva del cambio
lah levah del kambyo
gear shift

l'impianto stereo
leempyantoh stereo
car stereo

ROAD SIGNS

senso unico
senzoh ooneeko
one way

rotatoria
rotatorya
traffic circle

dare la precedenza
dareh lah prechedentsa
yield

divieto di sosta
deevyetoh dee sostah
no stopping

divieto di accesso
deevyetoh dee atchessoh
no entry

sosta vietata
sostah vyetatah
no parking

limite di velocità
leemeeteh dee velocheetah
speed limit

pericolo
pereekoloh
hazard

l'autostrada
lowtostradah
highway

la bretella
lah bretellah
entrance/exit ramp

ON THE ROAD

il parchimetro
eel parkeemetroh
parking meter

il semaforo
eel semaforoh
traffic light

il vigile
eel veejeeleh
traffic policeman

la cartina
lah karteenah
map

l'attraversamento pedonale
latraversamentoh pedonaleh
pedestrian crossing

il telefono di emergenza
eel telefonoh dee emerjentsa
emergency phone

l'ingorgo stradale
leengorgoh stradahleh
traffic jam

il parcheggio per disabili
eel parkedjoh pehr deezabeelee
disabled parking

AT THE STATION

Where can I buy a ticket?	Dove posso acquistare un biglietto? *doveh possoh akweestareh oon beelyettoh*
Is there an automatic ticket machine?	C'è una biglietteria automatica? *che oonah beelyettereeya owtomateekah*

la biglietteria automatica
lah beelyetterya owtomateekah
automatic ticket machine

il biglietto
eel beelyettoh
ticket

Two tickets to…	Due biglietti per… *dooeh beelyettee pehr*
I'd like…	Vorrei… *vorray*
…a one-way ticket to…	…un biglietto di sola andata per… *oon beelyettoh dee solah andatah pehr*
…a return ticket to…	…un biglietto di andata e ritorno per… *oon beelyettoh dee andatah eh reetornoh pehr*
…a first class ticket	…un biglietto di prima classe *oon beelyettoh dee preemah klasseh*
…a standard class ticket	…un biglietto di classe economica *oon beelyettoh dee klasseh ekonomeekah*

I'd like to…	Vorrei… *vorray*
…reserve a seat	…prenotare un posto *prenotareh oon postoh*
…on the Eurostar to…	…sull'Eurostar per… *soolehoorostar pehr*
…book a sleeper berth	…prenotare una cuccetta *prenotareh oonah koochettah*
Is there a reduction…?	C'è una riduzione… *che oonah reedootsyoneh*
…for children?	…per i bambini? *pehr ee bambeenee*
…for students?	…per gli studenti? *pehr lyee stoodentee*
…for senior citizens?	…per gli anziani? *pehr lyee antsyanee*
Is there a dining car?	C'è una carrozza ristorante? *che oonah karrodza reestoranteh*
Is it a fast/slow train?	È un treno rapido/locale? *eh oon trenoh rapeedoh/ lokaleh*
Do I stamp the ticket before boarding?	Devo vidimare il biglietto prima di salire in carrozza? *devoh veedeemareh eel beelyettoh preemah dee saleereh een karrodza*

You may hear…

- Il treno parte dal binario…
  eel trenoh parteh dal beenaryo
  The train leaves from platform…

- Deve cambiare treno.
  deveh kambyareh trenoh
  You must change trains.

TRAVELING BY TRAIN

Do you have a timetable?	Ha un orario? *ah oon oraryo*
What time is...	A che ora è... *ah ke orah eh*
...the next train to...?	...il prossimo treno per...? *eel prosseemoh trenoh pehr*
...the last train to...?	...l'ultimo treno per...? *loolteemoh trenoh pehr*
Which platform does it leave from?	Da quale binario parte? *dah kwaleh beenaryo parteh*
What time does it arrive in...?	A che ora arriva a...? *a ke orah arreevah ah*
How long does it take?	Quanto tempo ci impiega? *kwantoh tempoh chee eempyegah*
Is this the train for...?	È questo il treno per...? *eh kwestoh eel trenoh pehr*
Is this the right platform for...?	È questo il binario giusto per...? *eh kwestoh eel beenaryo jewstoh pehr*
Where is platform three?	Dov'è il binario tre? *doveh eel beenaryo treh*
Does this train stop at...?	Questo treno ferma a...? *kwestoh trenoh fermah ah*

You may hear...

- **Deve vidimare il biglietto.**
  deveh veedeemareh eel beelyettoh
  You must validate your ticket.

- **Usi la macchinetta gialla.**
  oozee lah makeenettah jallah
  Use the yellow machine.

Where do I change for…?	Dove devo cambiare per…? *doveh devoh kambyareh pehr*
Is this seat free?	È libero questo posto? *eh leeberoh kwestoh postoh*
I've reserved this seat	Ho prenotato questo posto *oh prenotatoh kwestoh postoh*
Do I get off here?	Devo scendere qui? *devoh shendereh kwee*
Where is the subway station?	Dov'è la stazione della metropolitana? *doveh lah statsyoneh dellah metropoleetanah*
Which line goes to…?	Quale linea arriva a…? *kwaleh leeneah arrivah ah*
How many stops is it?	Quante fermate sono? *kwanteh fermateh sonoh*

l'atrio
latryo
concourse

il treno
eel trenoh
train

la carrozza ristorante
lah karrodzah reestoranteh
dining car

la cuccetta
lah kootchettah
sleeper car

BUSES

When is the next bus to…?	Quando parte il prossimo autobus per…? *kwandoh parteh eel prosseemoh owtoboos pehr*
What is the fare to…?	Quanto costa un biglietto per…? *kwantoh kostah oon beelyettoh pehr*
Where is the bus stop?	Dov'è la fermata dell'autobus? *doveh lah fermatah del owtoboos*
Is this the bus stop for…	È questa la fermata dell'autobus per…? *eh kwestah lah fermatah del owtoboos pehr*
Where can I buy a ticket?	Dove posso acquistare un biglietto? *doveh possoh akweestareh oon beelyettoh*
Can I pay on the bus?	Posso pagare sull'autobus? *possoh pagareh soolowtoboos*
Which buses go to the city center?	Quali autobus raggiungono il centro? *kwalee owtoboos radjewngonoh eel chentroh*
Will you tell me when to get off?	Mi può dire quando devo scendere? *mee pwo deereh kwandoh devoh shendereh*

l'autobus
lowtoboos
bus

la stazione degli autobus
lah statsyoneh delyee owtoboos
bus station

TAXIS

Can I order a taxi?	Dove posso richiedere un taxi? *doveh possoh reekyedereh oon taxi*
I want a taxi to…	Desidero un taxi per… *deseederoh oon taxi pehr*
Can you take me to…	Mi può portare a/in… *mee pwo portareh ah/een*
Is it far?	È lontano? *eh lontanoh*
How much will it cost?	Quanto costa? *kwantoh kostah*
Can you drop me here?	Mi può far scendere qui? *mee pwo far shendereh kwee*
What do I owe you?	Quanto le devo? *kwantoh leh devoh*
I don't have any change	Non ho spiccioli *non oh spcetchyolee*
Keep the change	Tenga il resto *tengah eel restoh*
Please, may I have a receipt	Potrei avere la ricevuta, per favore *potray avereh lah reechevootah pehr favoreh*
Please wait for me	Mi aspetti, per favore *mee aspeteeh pehr favoreh*

il taxi
eel taxee
taxi

BOATS

Are there any boat trips?	Ci sono navi in partenza? *chee sonoh navee een partentsa*
Where does the boat leave from?	Dove parte la nave? *doveh parteh lah naveh*
When is...	Quando parte... *kwandoh parteh*
...the next boat to...?	...la prossima nave per...? *lah prosseemah naveh pehr*
...the first boat?	...la prima nave? *lah preemah naveh*
...the last boat?	...l'ultima nave? *loolteemah naveh*
I'd like two tickets for...	Vorrei due biglietti per... *vorray dooeh beelyettee pehr*
...the cruise	...la crociera *lah crotchyerah*

il traghetto
eel tragettoh
ferry

l'aliscafo
laleeskafoh
hydrofoil

lo yacht
loh yacht
yacht

l'hovercraft
lovercraft
hovercraft

| ...the river trip | ...la gita sul fiume
lah jeetah sool fewmeh |
| How much is it for... | Quanto costa per...
kwantoh kostah pehr |
| ...a car and two people? | ...un'automobile e due persone?
oon owtomobeeleh eh dooeh personeh |
| ...a family? | ...una famiglia?
oona fameelyah |
| ...a cabin | ...una cabina
oonah kabeenah |
| Can I buy a ticket on board? | Posso acquistare il biglietto a bordo?
possoh akweestareh eel beelyettoh ah bordoh |
| Is there wheelchair access? | C'è un accesso per disabili?
che oon atchessoh pehr deezabeelee |

il giubbotto di salvataggio
eel jewbottoh dee salvatadjoh
life jacket

il salvagente
eel salvajenteh
lifebuoy

il catamarano
eel katamaranoh
catamaran

Il motoscafo
eel motoscarfoh
motorboat

AIR TRAVEL

Which terminal do I need?	A quale terminal devo andare? *ah kwaleh terminahl devoh andareh*
Where do I check in?	Dove posso effettuare il check-in? *doveh possoh effetwareh eel check-in*
Where is…	Dove si trovano… *doveh see trovanoh*
…the arrivals hall?	…gli arrivi? *lyee arreevee*
…the departures hall?	…le partenze? *leh partentse*
…the boarding gate?	…le uscite d'imbarco? *leh oosheeteh deembarkoh*
I'm traveling…	Viaggio… *vyajoh*
…economy	…in classe economica *een klasseh ekonomeeka*

la sacca da viaggio
lah sakah dah vyajo
duffel

il pasto a bordo
eel pastoh ah bordoh
in-flight meal

il passaporto
eel passaportoh
passport

la carta d'imbarco
lah kartah deembarko
boarding pass

I'm checking in one suitcase	Desidero imbarcare un bagaglio *deseederoh eembarkareh oon bagalyo*
I packed it myself	Ho preparato io il bagaglio *oh preparatoh eeoh eel bagalyo*
I have one piece of hand luggage	Ho un unico bagaglio a mano *oh oon ooneeko bagalyo ah manoh*
How much is excess baggage?	A quanto ammonta il peso in eccesso? *ah kwantoh amontah eel pezoh een etchessoh*
Will a meal be served?	Sarà servito un pasto? *sarah serveetoh oon pastoh*
I'd like...	Vorrei... *vorray*
...a window seat	...un posto vicino al finestrino *oon postoh veecheenoh al feenestreenoh*
...an aisle seat	...un posto vicino al corridoio *oon postoh veecheenoh al koreedoyo*

You may hear...

- Il suo passaporto/biglietto, per favore.
  eel soowo passaportoh/ beelyettoh pehr favoreh
  Your passport/ticket, please.

- È sua questa borsa?
  eh soowa kwestah borsah
  Is this your bag?

AT THE AIRPORT

Here's my...	Ecco... *ekko*
...boarding pass	...la mia carta d'imbarco *la meeah karta deembarkoh*
...passport	...il mio passaporto *eel meeoh passaportoh*
Can I change some money?	Potrei cambiare del denaro? *potray kambyareh dehl denaroh?*

traveler's cheque
traveler's cheque
traveler's check

il controllo passaporti
eel kontrolloh passaportee
passport control

What is the exchange rate?	Qual è il tasso di cambio? *kwaleh eel tassoh dee kambyo*
Is the flight delayed?	Il volo è in ritardo? *eel voloh eh een reetardoh*
How late is it?	Quanto porta di ritardo? *kwantoh portah dee reetardoh*
Which gate does flight... leave from?	Qual è l'uscita del volo...? *kwaleh loosheetah del voloh*
What time do I board?	A che ora ci imbarchiamo? *ah keh orah chee eembarkyamoh*
When does the gate close?	Quando chiude l'uscita d'imbarco? *kwandoh kewdeh loosheetah deembarkoh*

Where are the luggage carts?	Dove sono i carrelli? *doveh sonoh ee karrelee*
Here is the claim tag	Ecco la ricevuta dei bagagli *ekko lah reechevootah day bagalye*
I can't find my baggage	Non trovo i miei bagagli *non trovoh ee myayee bagalye*

il negozio duty-free
eel negotsyo dootee free
duty-free shop

il pilota
eel peelotah
pilot

l'assistente di volo
lasseestenteh dee voloh
flight attendant

l'aeroplano
lahehroplahnoh
airplane

banco del check-in
banko del chek een
check-in desk

il ritiro bagagli
eel reeteeroh bagalyee
baggage claim

EATING OUT

It is not difficult to eat well and inexpensively in Italy. You can choose from cafés and bars, which serve a variety of drinks, snacks, and light meals, *osterie* and *trattorie* (small family-run restaurants that serve local and traditional dishes) and *pizzerie* (for pizzas and pasta). If you want a gastronomic meal in more formal surroundings, you can eat at more expensive *ristorante* but you may have to book in advance at the popular ones.

MAKING A RESERVATION

I'd like to book a table…	Vorrei prenotare un tavolo… *voray prenotareh oon tavoloh*
…for lunch/dinner	…per pranzo/cena *pehr prandzo/ chenah*
…for four people	…per quattro persone *pehr kwatroh personeh*
…for this evening	…per questa sera *pehr kwestah serah*
…for tomorrow at one	…per l'una di domani *pehr loonah dee domanee*
…for today	…per oggi *pehr ojee*
Do you have a table earlier/later?	Ha un tavolo prima/ più tardi? *ah oon tavoloh preemah/ pew tardee*
My name is…	Il cognome è… *eel konyomeh eh*
My telephone number is…	Il mio numero di telefono è… *eel meeoh noomeroh dee telefonoh eh*
Do you take credit cards?	Accettate carte di credito? *atchettateh karteh dee kredeetoh*
I have a reservation	Ho una prenotazione *oh oonah prenotatsyoneh*
in the name of…	a nome di… *ah nomeh dee*
We haven't booked	Non abbiamo prenotato *non abyamoh prenotatoh*
May we sit here?	Possiamo sederci qui? *possyamoh sederchee kwee*
We'd like to eat outside	Vorremmo mangiare fuori *vorremoh manjareh fworee*

ORDERING A MEAL

May we see the menu?	Possiamo vedere il menù? *possyamoh vedereh eel menoo*
...the wine list?	...la carta dei vini? *lah kartah day veenee*
Do you have...	Ha... *ah*
...a set menu?	...un menù fisso? *oon menoo feesoh*
...a fixed-price menu?	...un menù a prezzo fisso? *oon menoo ah predzo feesoh*
...a children's menu?	...un menù per bambini? *oon menoo pehr bambeenee*
...an à la carte menu	...un menù alla carta? *oon menoo allah kartah*
What are today's specials?	Qual è la specialità del giorno? *kwaleh lah spechyaleetah del jornoh*
What is this?	Cos'è questo/a? *kozeh kwestoh/ah*

You may hear...

- **Ha prenotato?**
  ah prenotatoh
  Do you have a reservation?

- **A nome di?**
  ah nomeh dee
  In what name?

- **Si sieda per favore**
  see syedah pehr favoreh
  Please be seated

- **Vuole ordinare?**
  vwoleh ordeenareh
  Are you ready to order?

Are there any vegetarian dishes?	Avete dei piatti vegetariani? *aveteh day pyatee vejetaryanee*
I can't eat…	Non posso mangiare… *non possoh manjareh*
…dairy foods	…i latticini *ee latteecheenee*
…nuts	…la frutta secca *lah frootah sekah*
…wheat	…il frumento *eel froomentoh*
To drink, I'll have…	Da bere, vorrei… *dah bereh vorray*
May we have…	Possiamo avere… *possyamoh avereh*
…some water	…dell'acqua? *delakwa*
…some bread?	…del pane? *del paneh*
…the dessert menu?	…il menù dei dolci? *eel menoo day dolchee*

Reading the menu

• **Gli antipasti** *lyee anteepastee*	Starters
• **I primi** *ee preemee*	First courses
• **I secondi** *ee sekondee*	Main courses
• **I contorni** *ee kontornee*	Vegetables
• **I formaggi** *ee formadjee*	Cheeses
• **I dolci** *ee dolchee*	Desserts

COMPLAINING

I didn't order this	Non ho ordinato questo/a *non oh ordeenatoh kwestoh/ah*
When is our food coming?	Quando arriva il cibo? *kwandoh arreevah eel cheeboh*
We can't wait any longer	Non possiamo aspettare oltre *non possyamoh aspettareh oltreh*

PAYING

The check, please	Il conto, per favore *eel kontoh pehr favoreh*
Can we pay separately?	Possiamo pagare separatamente? *possyamoh pagareh separatamenteh*
Can I have...	Posso avere... *possoh avereh*
...a receipt?	...la ricevuta? *lah reechevootah*
...an itemized bill?	...una ricevuta dettagliata? *oonah reechevootah detalyatah*
Is service included?	Il servizio è incluso? *eel serveetsyo eh eenkloozoh*

You may hear...

- **Non accettiamo carte di credito.**
  non atchetyamoh karteh dee kredeetoh
  We don't take credit cards.

- **Digiti il PIN.**
  deejeetee eel peen
  Please enter your PIN.

DISHES AND CUTLERY

il piattino
eel pyateenoh
side plate

la scodella
lah skodellah
bowl

il pepe
eel pepeh
pepper

il sale
eel saleh
salt

la tazza e il piattino
lah tadza eh eel pyateenoh
cup and saucer

il cucchiaino
eel kookyaeenoh
teaspoon

il bicchiere
eel beekyereh
glass

il cucchiaio
eel kookyayo
dessert spoon

il coltello
eel koltelloh
knife

il tovagliolo
eel tovalyoloh
napkin

la forchetta
lah forkettah
fork

il piatto piano
eel pyato pyanoh
dinner plate

AT THE CAFÉ OR BAR

The menu, please	Il menù, per favore *eel menooh pehr favoreh*
Do you have…?	Ha…? *ah*
What fruit juices/herbal teas do you have?	Quali succhi di frutta/tisane ha? *kwalee sookee dee frootah/ teezaneh ah*
I'd like…	Vorrei… *vorray*

un caffellatte
oon kaffelatteh
white coffee

un caffè
oon kaffeh
black coffee

un espresso
oon espressoh
espresso

un cappuccino
oon kapootcheenoh
cappuccino

You may hear…

- **Cosa desidera?**
  kozah deseederah
  What would you like?

- **Altro?**
  altroh
  Anything else?

- **Prego.**
  pregoh
  You're welcome.

un tè al latte
oon teh al latteh
tea with milk

un tè al limone
oon teh al leemoneh
tea with lemon

un tè alla menta
oon teh allah mentah
mint tea

un tè verde
oon teh verdeh
green tea

una camomilla
oonah kamomeelah
camomile tea

una cioccolata calda
oonah chokolatah kaldah
hot chocolate

A bottle of…	Una bottiglia di… *oonah botteelya dee*
A glass of…	Un bicchiere di… *oon beekyereh dee*
A cup of…	Una tazza di… *oonah tadza dee*
With lemon/milk	con limone/latte *kon leemoneh/latteh*
Another…please	Un altro/a…per favore *oon altroh/ah…pehr favoreh*
The same again, please	Me ne porta ancora, per favore *meh neh portah ankorah pehr favoreh*

CAFÉ AND BAR DRINKS

un caffè shakerato
oon kaffeh shakeratoh
iced coffee

una spremuta d'arancia
oonah spremootah daranchya
fresh orange juice

un succo di mela
oon sookoh dee melah
apple juice

un succo di ananas
oon sookoh dee ananas
pineapple juice

un succo di pomodoro
oon sookoh dee pomodoroh
tomato juice

un succo d'uva
oon sookoh doovah
grape juice

una limonata
oonah leemonatah
lemonade

un crodino
oon krodeenoh
Crodino

una coca cola
oonah kokakolah
cola

un prosecco
oon prosekoh
sparkling wine

acqua minerale
akwa meeneraleh
mineral water

una grappa
oonah grappah
Grappa

una birra
oonah beerrah
beer

un campari
oon kamparee
Campari

un vino rosso
oon veenoh rossoh
red wine

un vino bianco
oon veenoh byankoh
white wine

You may hear...

- **In bottiglia o alla spina?**
  een botteelya oh allah speenah
  Bottled or draft?

- **Liscia o gassata?**
  leesha oh gassatah
  Still or sparkling?

- **Con ghiaccio?**
  kon gyachyo
  With ice?

BAR SNACKS

un tramezzino
oon tramedzeenoh
sandwich

un panino
oon paneenoh
panino

le olive
leh oliveh
olives

le noccioline
leh notcholeeneh
nuts

il condimento
eel kondimentoh
dressing

l'insalata
leensalatah
salad

i biscotti
ee beeskottee
biscotti

la bruschetta
lah brooskettah
bruschetta

il gelato
eel jelatoh
ice cream

i maritozzi
ee mareetodzee
cream buns

FAST FOOD

May I have…
Posso avere…
possoh avereh

…to eat in/carry out
…da mangiare qui/da portare via
dah manjareh kwee/dah portareh vee-ah

un hamburger
oon amboorger
hamburger

un hamburger di pollo
oon amboorger dee polloh
chicken burger

una piadina arrotolata
oonah pyadeenah arotolatah
wrap

un hot dog
oon otdog
hot dog

un kebab
oon kebab
kebab

le patatine
leh patateeneh
French fries

il pollo fritto
eel polloh freetoh
fried chicken

la pizza
lah peedza
pizza

BREAKFAST

May I have…	Posso avere… *possoh avereh*
…some milk	…del latte? *del latteh*
…some sugar	dello zucchero? *delloh tsookeroh*
…some artificial sweetener	…del dolcificante? *del dolcheefeekanteh*
…some butter	…del burro? *del booroh*
…some jam?	…della marmellata? *dellah marmellatah*
…some salt/pepper?	…del sale/del pepe? *del saleh/del pehpeh*

un caffè
oon kaffeh
coffee

un tè
oon teh
tea

una cioccolata calda
oonah chokolatah kaldah
hot chocolate

una spremuta d'arancia
oonah spremootah daranchya
orange juice

un succo di mela
oon sookoh dee melah
apple juice

il pane
eel paneh
bread

un cornetto
oon kornettoh
croissant

un cornetto al cioccolato
oon kornettoh al chokolatoh
chocolate croissant

la marmellata
lah marmellatah
marmalade

un panino
oon paneenoh
bread roll

le uova strapazzate
leh wovah strapadzateh
scrambled eggs

il miele
eel myeleh
honey

l'uovo in camicia
lwovoh een kameecha
poached egg

l'uovo sodo
lwovoh sodoh
boiled egg

la frutta fresca
lah frootah freskah
fresh fruit

lo yoghurt alla frutta
loh yogoort allah frootah
fruit yogurt

FIRST COURSES

la minestra
lah meenestrah
soup

il brodo
eel brodoh
broth

la zuppa di pesce
lah tsoopah dee pesheh
fish soup

il minestrone
eel meenestroneh
minestrone

gli gnocchi
lyee nyokee
gnocchi

la frittata
lah freetatah
omelet

la bresaola
lah bresaolah
bresaola

il risotto
eel reezottoh
risotto

il prosciutto crudo
eel proshewtoh kroodoh
cured ham

i gamberi alla griglia
ee gamberee allah greelya
grilled shrimp

l'antipasto di mare
lanteepastoh dee mareh
seafood antipasto

le sarde al saor
leh sardeh al saor
Venetian-style sardines

l'antipasto misto
lanteepastoh meestoh
mixed antipasto

l'antipasto freddo
lanteepastoh freddoh
antipasto of cold meats

gli spaghetti alla vongole
lyee spagetee alla vongoleh
spaghetti with clams

gli spaghetti alla carbonara
lyee spagetee alla karbonara
spaghetti carbonara

gli spaghetti alla bolognese
lyee spagetee alla bolonyeseh
spaghetti bolognese

la bagna cauda
lah banya cowdah
hot anchovy dip

i cannelloni
ee kannellonee
cannelloni

i tortelloni
ee tortellonee
tortelloni

MAIN COURSES

I would like...	Vorrei... *vorray*
...the chicken	...il pollo *eel polloh*
...the duck	...l'anatra *lanatrah*
...the lamb	...l'agnello *lanyelloh*
...the pork	...il maiale *eel mayaleh*
...the beef	...il manzo *eel mandzo*
...the steak	...la bistecca *lah beestekkah*
...the veal	...il vitello *eel veeteloh*
...the liver	...il fegato *eel fegatoh*
roast	arrosto *arrostoh*
baked	al forno *al fornoh*
grilled	alla griglia *allah greelya*
on skewers	allo spiedo *alloh spyedoh*

You may see...

i frutti di mare
ee frootee dee mareh
seafood

il pesce
eel pesheh
fish

You may hear...

• **Come desidera la bistecca?**
komeh deseederah lah beestekkah
How do you like your steak?

• **Al sangue, a cottura media o ben cotta?**
al sangweh, ah kottoorah medya oh ben kottah
Rare, medium rare, or well done?

barbecued	al barbecue *al barbekew*
poached	in camicia *een kameechya*
boiled	lesso/sodo *lessoh/sodoh*
fried	fritto *freetoh*
pan-fried/sautéed	in padella/saltato *een padellah/saltatoh*
stuffed	farcito *farcheetoh*
stewed	stufato *stoofatoh*
...with Parmesan cheese	...con il parmigiano *kon eel parmeejanoh*

il pollame
eel pollameh
poultry

la carne
lah karneh
meat

SALADS AND SIDE DISHES

l'insalata verde
leensalatah verdeh
green salad

l'insalata mista
leensalatah meestah
mixed salad

il radicchio alla griglia
eel radeekkyo allah greelya
grilled radicchio

le verdure al vapore
leh verdooreh al vaporeh
steamed vegetables

il riso
eel reezoh
rice

la pasta
lah pastah
pasta

le patatine fritte
leh patateeneh freeteh
French fries

gli spinaci
lyee speenachee
spinach

gli asparagi
lyee asparajee
asparagus

la polenta
lah polentah
polenta

DESSERTS

la mousse di cioccolato
lah moos dee chokolatoh
chocolate mousse

la cassata
lah kassatah
cassata

la crostata di nocciole
lah krostatah dee nochyoleh
hazelnut tart

la crostata di ricotta
lah krostatah dee reekottah
ricotta tart

il sorbetto
eel sorbettoh
sorbet

il gelato
eel jelatoh
ice cream

il tiramisù
eel teerameesoo
tiramisù

la torta
lah tortah
cake

la crostata di frutta
lah krostatah dee frootah
fruit tart

lo zabaglione
loh tsabalyoneh
zabaglione

PLACES TO STAY

Italy has a wide range of places to stay, depending on your personal preference and budget. These range from elegant hotels in former *palazzi* to smaller *alberghi*, *locande* (one-star hotels), and family-run *pensioni*. If you want the option to cook for yourself, however, you can choose to rent a seaside apartment or a country villa, or find a campsite to park your camper or put up your tent.

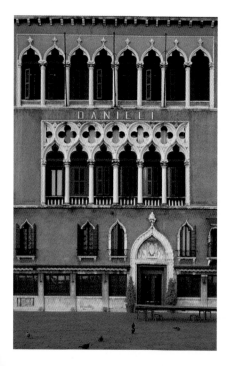

MAKING A RESERVATION

I'd like...	Vorrei... *vorray*
...to make a reservation	...fare una prenotazione *fareh oonah prenotatsyoneh*
...a double room	...una camera doppia *oonah kamerah doppya*
...a room with two twin beds	...una camera a due letti *oonah kamerah ah dooeh lettee*
...a single room	...una camera singola *oonah kamerah seengolah*
...a family room	...una camera familiare *oonah kamerah fameelyareh*
...a disabled person's room	...una camera per disabili *oonah kamerah pehr deezabeelee*
...with a bath/shower	...con bagno/doccia *kon banyo/dotchya*
...with a sea view	...con vista sul mare *kon veestah sool mareh*
...with a balcony	...con balcone *kon balkoneh*
...for two nights	...per due notti *pehr dooeh nottee*
...for a week	...per una settimana *pehr oonah setteemanah*
Is breakfast included?	La colazione è inclusa? *lah kolatsyoneh eh eenkloosah*
How much is it...	Quanto costa... *kwantoh kostah*
...per night?	...a notte? *ah notteh*
...per week?	...alla settimana? *allah setteemanah*

CHECKING IN

I have a reservation in the name of…	Ho una prenotazione a nome di… *oh oonah prenotatsyoneh ah nomeh dee*
Do you have…	Ha… *ah*

un facchino
oon fakeenoh
a porter

gli ascensori
lyee ashenzoree
elevators

il servizio in camera
eel serveetsyo een kamerah
room service

il mini bar
eel meenee bar
mini bar

I'd like…	Vorrei… *vorray*
…the keys for room…	…le chiavi della camera… *leh kyavee dellah kamerah*
…a wake-up call at…	…la sveglia alle… *lah svelya alleh*
What time is…	A che ora servite… *ah ke orah serveeteh*
…breakfast?	…la colazione? *lah kolatsyoneh*
…dinner?	…la cena? *lah chenah*

IN YOUR ROOM

Do you have…	Ha… *ah*
another…	un altro/a… *oon altroh/ah*
some more…	altri/e… *altree/eh*

i cuscini
ee koosheenee
pillows

le coperte
leh koperteh
blankets

una lampadina
oonah lampadeenah
a light bulb

un adattatore
oon adatatoreh
an adapter

I've lost my key   Ho perso la mia chiave
oh persoh lah meeah kiaveh

You may hear…

- Il suo numero di camera è…
  eel soo-oh noomeroh dee kamerah eh
  Your room number is…

- Ecco la sua chiave.
  ekko lah sooah kiaveh
  Here is your key.

IN THE HOTEL

The room is…	La camera è… *lah kamerah e*
…too hot	…troppo calda *troppoh kaldah*
…too cold	…troppo fredda *troppoh freddah*
…too small	…troppo piccola *troppoh peekolah*

il termostato
eel termostatoh
thermostat

il radiatore
eel radyatoreh
radiator

la camera singola
lah kamerah seengolah
single room

la camera doppia
lah kamerah doppya
double room

il numero della camera
eel noomeroh dellah kamerah
room number

il bollitore
eel bolleetoreh
tea kettle

The window won't open	La finestra non si apre *lah feenestrah non see apreh*
The TV doesn't work	Il televisore non funziona *eel televeezoreh non funtsyonah*

l'appendiabiti
lappendeeabeetee
coat hanger

il televisore
eel televeezoreh
television

la veneziana
lah venetsyanah
venetian blind

il telecomando
eel telekomandoh
remote control

CHECKING OUT

When do I have to vacate the room?	Quando devo lasciare la stanza? *kwandoh devoh lasheeareh lah standza*
Is there a porter to carry my bags?	C'è un facchino per portare le mie valigie? *che oon fakkeenoh pehr portareh leh meeye valeejeh*
May I have the bill, please?	Posso avere il conto? *possoh avereh eel kontoh*
May I pay…	Posso pagare… *possoh pagareh*
…by credit card?	…con la carta di credito? *kon lah kartah dee kredeetoh*
…cash?	…in contanti? *een kontantee*
I'd like a receipt	Vorrei la ricevuta *vorray lah reechevootah*

IN THE BATHROOM

la vasca da bagno
lah vaska dah banyo
bathtub

il bidet
eel beedeh
bidet

il sapone
eel saponeh
soap

gli asciugamani
lyee ashewgamanee
towels

l'accappatoio
lakappatoyo
bathrobe

il bagnoschiuma
eel banyoskewmah
bubble bath

il docciaschiuma
eel dotchyaskwemah
shower gel

il deodorante
eel dehodoranteh
deodorant

la crema per il corpo
lah kremah pehr eel korpoh
body lotion

il dentifricio
eel denteefreechyo
toothpaste

lo spazzolino da denti
loh spatsoleenoh dah dentee
toothbrush

il colluttorio
eel koolootoryo
mouthwash

il rasoio elettrico
eel rasoyo eletreeko
electric razor

la schiuma da barba
lah skewmah dah barbah
shaving foam

il rasoio
eel rasoyo
razor

l'asciugacapelli
lashewgakapellee
hair dryer

lo shampoo
loh shampoh
shampoo

il balsamo
eel balsamoh
conditioner

il tagliaunghie
eel talyaoongye
nail clippers

le forbici per unghie
leh forbeechee pehr oongye
nail scissors

SELF-CATERING

May we have...	Possiamo avere... *possyamoh avereh*
...the key, please?	...la chiave, per favore? *lah kiaveh pehr favoreh*
...an extra bed?	...un letto extra? *oon lettoh extrah*
...a child's bed?	...un lettino? *oon letteenoh*

il seggiolone
eel sedjoloneh
high chair

il lettino
eel leteenoh
crib

...more cutlery, dishes	...più posate, stoviglie *pew posateh stoveelye*
Where is...	Dov'è... *doveh*
...the fusebox?	...la scatola dei fusibili? *lah skatolah day fooseebeelee*
...the water valve?	...il rubinetto d'arresto? *eel roobeenettoh darrestoh*
...the nearest store?	...il negozio più vicino? *eel negotsyo pew veecheenoh*
Do you do babysitting?	Offrite un servizio di babysitting? *offreeteh oon serveetsyo dee babyseetteeng*
How does the heating work?	Come funziona il riscaldamento? *komeh foontsyonah eel reeskaldamentoh*

Is there…	C'è… *che*
…air conditioning?	…l'aria condizionata? *larya kondeetsyonatah*
…central heating?	…il riscaldamento centralizzato? *eel reeskaldamentoh chentraleedzatoh*

il ventilatore
eel venteelatoreh
fan

il termoconvettore
eel termokonverteetoreh
space heater

When does the cleaner come?	Quando passa l'addetto alle pulizie? *kwandoh passah ladettoh alleh pooleetsye*
Where do I put the garbage?	Dove posso buttare l'immondizia? *doveh possoh bootareh leemondeetsyah*
Do you take pets?	Accettate animali domestici? *atchettateh aneemalee domesteechee*

il cane
eel kaneh
dog

IN THE VILLA

Is there an inventory?	C'è un inventario? *che oon eenventaryo*
Where is this item?	Dove si trova questo articolo? *doveh see trovah kwestoh arteekoloh*
I need…	Ho bisogno di… *oh beezonyo dee*
…an extension cord	…una prolunga *oonah proloongah*
…a flashlight	…una torcia *oonah torchya*
…matches	…dei fiammiferi *day fyameeferee*

il forno a microonde
eel fornoh ah meekrohondeh
microwave

il ferro da stiro
eel ferroh dah steeroh
iron

l'asse da stiro
lasseh dah steeroh
ironing board

il mocio e il secchio
eel mochyo eh eel sekkyo
mop and bucket

la paletta e la scopetta
lah palettah eh lah skopettah
dust pan and brush

il detersivo
eel deterseevoh
detergent

PROBLEM SOLVING

The shower doesn't work	La doccia non funziona *lah dotchya non foontsyonah*
The toilet is leaking	Il water perde acqua *eel vater perdeh akwa*
Can you fix it today?	Può aggiustarlo oggi? *pwo adjewstarloh ojee*
There's no...	Non c'è... *non che*
...electricity/gas	...elettricità/gas *eletreecheetah/gas*
...water	...acqua *akwa*

la lavatrice
lah lavatreeche
washing machine

il frigorifero
eel freegoreeferoh
refrigerator

la pattumiera
lah patoomyerah
garbage can

il lucchetto e la chiave
eel lookettoh eh lah kiaveh
lock and key

il rivelatore di fumo
eel reevelatoreh dee foomoh
smoke alarm

l'estintore
lesteentoreh
fire extinguisher

KITCHEN EQUIPMENT

l'apriscatole
lapreeskatoleh
can opener

l'apribottiglie
lapreeboteelyeh
bottle opener

il cavatappi
eel kavatappee
corkscrew

il tagliere
eel talyehreh
cutting board

il coltello da cucina
eel koltelloh dah koocheenah
kitchen knife

lo sbucciatore
loh sbootchyatoreh
peeler

la frusta
lah froostah
whisk

il cucchiaio di legno
eel kookyayo dee lenyo
wooden spoon

la spatola
lah spatolah
spatula

la grattuggia
lah grattoojah
grater

il colapasta
eel kolapastah
colander

la padella
lah padellah
frying pan

la pentola
la pentolah
saucepan

la griglia
lah greelya
grill pan

la casseruola
lah kasserwolah
casserole dish

l'insalatiera
leensalatyerah
mixing bowl

il frullatore
eel froolatoreh
blender

la teglia da forno
lah telya dah fornoh
cookie sheet

i guanti da forno
ee gwantee dah fornoh
oven mitts

il grembiule
eel grembewleh
apron

CAMPING

Where is the nearest...	Dov'è il più vicino... *doveh eel pew veecheenoh*
...campground?	...campeggio? *kampedjoh*
...camper van site?	...campeggio per camper? *kampedjoh pehr kamper*
Can we camp here?	Possiamo accamparci qui? *possyamoh akamparchee kwee*
Do you have any vacancies?	C'è posto disponibile? *che postoh deesponeebeeleh*
What is the charge...	Quanto costa... *kwantoh kostah*
...per night?	...per notte? *pehr notteh*
...per week?	...per settimana? *pehr setteemanah*
Does the price include...	Il costo include... *eel kostoh eenkloodeh*
...electricity?	...l'elettricità? *leletreecheetah*
...hot water?	...l'acqua calda? *lakwa kaldah*
We want to stay for...	Desideriamo rimanere per... *deseederyamoh reemanereh pehr*

il picchetto
eel peekkettoh
tent peg

la tenda
lah tendah
tent

la corda
lah kordah
guy rope

Can I rent...	Posso noleggiare... *possoh noledjareh*
...a tent?	...una tenda? *oonah tendah*
...a barbecue?	...un barbecue? *oon barbecue*
Where are...	Dove sono... *doveh sonoh*
...the toilets?	...i servizi? *ee serveetsee*
...the garbage cans?	...i bidoni dell'immondizia? *ee beedonee del eemondeetsya*
Are there...	Ci sono... *chee sonoh*
...showers?	...docce? *dotcheh*
...laundry facilities?	...servizi di lavanderia? *serveetsee dee lavanderya*
Is there...	C'è... *che*
...a swimming pool?	...una piscina? *oonah peesheenah*
...a store?	...un negozio? *oon negotsyo*

You may hear...

- **Non accendere il fuoco.**
  non atchendereh eel fwoko
  Don't light a fire.

- **Non bere l'acqua.**
  non bereh lakwa
  Don't drink the water.

AT THE CAMPSITE

il sacco a pelo
eel sakko ah peloh
sleeping bag

il materasso gonfiabile
eel materassoh gonfyabeeleh
air mattress

il bollitore
eel boleetoreh
camping kettle

il thermos
eel termos
vacuum flask

il fornello da campeggio
eel fornelloh dah kampedjoh
camping stove

il barbecue
eel barbecue
barbecue

il frigo portatile
eel freegoh portateeleh
cooler

l'acqua in bottiglia
lakwa een botteelya
bottled water

il cestino da picnic
eel chesteenoh dah picnic
picnic basket

il secchio
eel sekyo
bucket

il maglio
eel malyo
mallet

la bussola
lah boosolah
compass

la torcia
lah torchya
flashlight

la matassa di spago
lah matassah dee spagoh
ball of string

il filtro solare
eel feeltroh solareh
sunscreen

i cerotti
ee cherotee
adhesive bandage

gli scarponi da montagna
lye skarponee dah montanya
hiking boots

lo zaino
loh dzaeenoh
backpack

SHOPPING

In addition to shopping malls, supermarkets, and specialty stores, Italy has many picturesque open-air markets in town squares and on main streets where you can buy food, clothes, and even antiques relatively cheaply. Most stores are open between 8:30 a.m. and 12:30 p.m., and 3:30 p.m. to 7:30 p.m. from Tuesday to Saturday. However, many stores and groceries are closed on Monday mornings or all day Mondays.

IN THE STORE

I'm looking for…	Sto cercando… *stoh cherkandoh*
Do you have…?	Avete…? *aveteh*
I'm just looking	Sto solo guardando *stoh soloh gwardandoh*
I'm being helped	Mi stanno già servendo *mee stannoh jah servendoh*
Do you have any more of these?	Ne avete ancora? *eh aveteh ankorah*
How much is this?	Quanto costa questo? *wantoh kostah kwestoh*
Do you have anything cheaper?	Avete qualcosa di meno costoso? *aveteh kwalkosah dee menoh kostosoh*
I'll take this one	Prendo questo/a *prendoh kwestoh/ah*
Where can I pay?	Dove posso pagare? *doveh possoh pagareh*
I'll pay…	Desidero pagare… *deseederoh pagareh*
…in cash	…in contanti *een kontantee*
…by credit card	…con la carta di credito *kon lah kartah dee kredeetoh*
May I have a receipt?	Mi può fare lo scontrino? *mee pwo fareh loh skontreenoh?*
I'd like to exchange this	Vorrei cambiare questo/a *vorray kambyareh kwestoh/ah*

AT THE BANK

I'd like...	Desidero... *deseederoh*
...to make a withdrawal	...effettuare un prelievo *effettwareh oon prelyevoh*
...to deposit some money	...effettuare un deposito *effettwareh oon deposeetoh*
...to change some money	...cambiare del denaro *kambyareh del denaroh*
...into euros	...in euro *een ehooroh*
...into dollars	...in dollari *een dohlaree*
Here is my passport	Ecco il mio passaporto *ekko eel meeo passaportoh*
My name is...	Mi chiamo... *mee kiamoh*
My account number is...	Il mio numero di conto è... *eel meeo noomeroh dee kontoh eh*
My bank details are...	I miei dettagli bancari sono... *ee myayee dettalyee bankaree sonoh*

il tasso di cambio
eel tassoh dee kambyo
exchange rate

il travellers' cheque
eel travelers chek
traveler's check

il passaporto
eel passaportoh
passport

il denaro
eel denaroh
money

Do I have...	Devo... *devoh*
...to key in my PIN number?	...digitare il PIN? *deejeetareh eel peen*
...to sign here?	...firmare qui? *feermareh kwee*
The cash machine has eaten my card	Lo sportello bancomat ha preso la mia carta *loh sportelloh bankomat ah presoh luh meea kartah*
Can I cash a check?	Posso incassare un assegno? *possoh eenkassareh oon assenyo*
Has my money arrived yet?	È arrivato il mio denaro? *eh arreevatoh eel meeo denaroh*
When does the bank open/close?	Quando apre/chiude la banca? *kwandoh apreh/kewdeh lah bankah*

lo sportello bancomat
loh sportelloh bankomat
cash machine

il direttore della banca
eel deerettoreh dellah bankah
bank manager

la carta di credito
lah kartah dee kredeetoh
credit card

il libretto degli assegni
eel leebrettoh delyee assenyee
checkbook

STORES

la panetteria
lah panetterya
bakery

il fruttivendolo
eel frooteevendoloh
greengrocery

la gastronomia
lah gastronomya
delicatessen

la pescheria
lah peskerya
fish seller

il tabaccaio
eel tabakkayo
tobacco shop

la boutique
lah booteek
boutique

il negozio di dischi
eel negotsyo dee deeskee
record store

il negozio di mobili
eel negotsyo dee mobeelee
furniture store

la macelleria
lah machelerya
butcher's

la drogheria
lah drogerya
grocery store

il supermercato
eel soopermerkatoh
supermarket

la libreria
lah leebrerya
book store

il negozio di calzature
eel negotsyo dee kaltsatooreh
shoe store

la sartoria
lah sartorya
tailor's

la gioielleria
lah joyellerya
jewelery store

la ferramenta
lah ferramentah
hardware store

AT THE MARKET

I would like…	Desidero… *deseederoh*
How much is this?	Quanto costa? *kwantoh kostah*
What's the price per kilo?	Quanto costa al chilo? *kwantoh kostah al keeloh*
It's too expensive	È troppo caro *eh troppoh karoh*
Do you have anything cheaper?	Avete qualcosa di meno caro? *aveteh kwalkosah dee menoh karoh*
That's fine, I'll take it	Va bene, lo prendo *vah beneh loh prendoh*
I'll take two kilos	Me ne dia due chili *meh neh dya dooeh keelee*
A kilo of…	Un chilo di… *oon keeloh dee*
Half a kilo of…	Mezzo chilo di… *medzo keeloh dee*
A little more, please	Un po' di più, per favore *oon poh dee pew pehr favoreh*
May I taste it?	Posso assaggiarlo/a? *possoh assadjarloh/ah*
That will be all, thank you	È tutto, la ringrazio *eh tootoh lah reengratsyo*

You may hear…

- **Posso aiutarla?**
  possoh ayewtarlah
  May I help you?

- **Quanto ne vuole?**
  kwantoh neh vwoleh
  How much would you like?

IN THE SUPERMARKET

Where is/are…	Dov'è/dove sono… *doveh/doveh sonoh*
…the frozen foods	…i surgelati? *ee soorjelatee*
…the beverage aisle?	…la corsia delle bibite? *lah korsya delleh beebeeteh*
…the checkout?	…la cassa? *lah kassah*

il carrello
eel karrelloh
cart

il cestino
eel chesteenoh
basket

I'm looking for…	Sto cercando… *stoh cherkandoh*
Do you have any more?	Ne avete ancora? *neh aveteh ankorah*
Is this reduced?	È scontato? *eh skontatoh*
What is the sell-by date?	Qual è la data di scadenza? *kwaleh lah datah dee skadentsa*
Where do I pay?	Dove posso pagare? *doveh possoh pagareh*
Shall I key in my PIN?	Devo digitare il PIN? *devoh deejeetareh eel peen*
May I have a bag?	Posso avere un sacchetto? *possoh avereh oon sakettoh*
Can you help me pack	Mi può aiutare a riempire i sacchetti? *mee pwo ayewtareh ah ryempeereh ee sakettee*

FRUIT

l'arancia
laranchya
orange

il limone
eel leemoneh
lemon

il limone verde
eel leemoneh verdeh
lime

il pompelmo
eel pompelmoh
grapefruit

la pesca
lah peskah
peach

la pescanoce
lah peskanocheh
nectarine

l'albicocca
lalbeekokkah
apricot

la prugna
lah proonya
plum

la ciliegia
lah cheelyeja
cherry

il mirtillo
eel meerteeloh
blueberry

la fragola
lah fragolah
strawberry

il lampone
eel lamponeh
raspberry

il melone
eel meloneh
melon

l'uva
loovah
grapes

la banana
lah bananah
banana

la melagrana
lah melagranah
pomegranate

la mela
lah melah
apple

la pera
lah perah
pear

l'ananas
lananas
pineapple

il mango
eel mangoh
mango

VEGETABLES

la patata
lah patatah
potato

la carota
lah karotah
carrot

il peperone
eel peperoneh
pepper

il peperoncino
eel peperoncheenoh
chili

la melanzana
lah melandzanah
eggplant

il pomodoro
eel pomodoroh
tomato

la cipollina
lah cheepoleenah
scallion

il porro
eel porroh
leek

la cipolla
lah cheepolah
onion

l'aglio
lalyo
garlic

il fungo
eel foongoh
mushroom

la zucchina
lah dzookeenah
zucchini

il cetriolo
eel chetryoloh
cucumber

i fagiolini
ee fajoleenee
French bean

i piselli
ee peesellee
garden peas

il sedano
eel sedanoh
celery

gli spinaci
lyee speenachee
spinach

il broccolo
eel brokkoloh
broccoli

il cavolo
eel kavoloh
cabbage

la lattuga
lah latoogah
lettuce

MEAT AND POULTRY

May I have…	Posso avere…
	possoh avereh
…a slice of…?	…una fetta di…?
	oonah fettah dee
…a piece of…?	…un pezzo di…?
	oon pedzo dee

il prosciutto cotto
eel proshewtoh kottoh
cooked ham

il prosciutto crudo
eel proshewtoh kroodoh
cured ham

la bistecca
lah beestekka
steak

il filetto
eel feelettoh
fillet

il salame di cinghiale
eel salameh dee cheengyaleh
wild boar salami

la carne tritata
lah karneh treetatah
ground beef

il pollo
eel polloh
chicken

il rognone
eel ronyoneh
kidney

FISH AND SHELLFISH

la sogliola
lah solyolah
sole

eel calamaro
eel kalamaroh
squid

il merluzzo
eel merloodzo
cod

la spigola
lah speegolah
sea bass

il sarago
eel saragoh
sea bream

la sardina
lah sardeenah
sardine

il granchio
eel grankyo
crab

l'aragosta
laragostah
lobster

il gambero
eel gamberoh
shrimp

la capasanta
lah kapasantah
scallop

BREAD AND CAKES

il panino
eel paneenoh
roll

il pan marino
eel pan mareenoh
rosemary bread

il pane casalingo
eel paneh kasaleengoh
loaf of bread

i grissini
ee greeseenee
breadsticks

il cornetto
eel kornettoh
croissant

la focaccia
lah fokatchya
foccaccia

la crostata al limone
lah krostatah al leemoneh
lemon tart

la torta al cioccolato
lah tortah al chokolatoh
chocolate cake

il panettone
eel panettoneh
panettone

il panforte
eel panforteh
panforte

DAIRY PRODUCE

il latte intero
eel lateh eenteroh
whole milk

parzialmente scremato
partsyalmenteh skrematoh
skim milk

la panna
lah pannah
cream

la ricotta
lah reekottah
ricotta

lo yoghurt
loh yogoort
yogurt

il burro
eel booroh
butter

il provolone
eel provoloneh
Provolone

il parmigiano
eel parmeejanoh
Parmesan cheese

la mozzarella
lah mozzarellah
mozzarella

il pecorino
eel pekoreenoh
Pecorino

NEWSPAPERS AND MAGAZINES

Do you have...	Avete... *aveteh*
...a book of stamps?	...un carnet di francobolli? *oon karneh dee frankobollee*
...airmail stamps?	...francobolli di posta aerea? *frankobollee dee postah aehrehah*
...a box of envelopes?	...una confezione di buste? *oonah konfetsyoneh dee boosteh*

la cartolina
lah kartoleenah
postcard

i francobolli
ee frankobolee
stamps

la matita
lah mateetah
pencil

la penna
lah pennah
pen

You may hear...

- **Quale desidera?**
  kwaleh deseederah
  Which would you like?

- **Mi può dire la sua età?**
  mee pwo deereh lah sooa etah
  How old are you?

- **Ha la carta d'identità?**
  ah lah kartah deedenteetah
  Do you have ID?

I'd like…	Vorrei… *vorray*
…a pack of cigarettes	…un pacchetto di sigarette *oon pakkettoh dee seegaretteh*
…a box of matches	…una scatola di cerini *oonah skatolah dee chereenee*

del tabacco
del tabakkoh
tobacco

l'accendino
latchendeenoh
lighter

le gomme da masticare
leh gommeh dah masteekareh
chewing gum

le caramelle
leh karamelleh
candy

il quotidiano
eel kwoteedyanoh
newspaper

la rivista
lah reeveestah
magazine

i fumetti
ee foomettee
comic

le matite colorate
leh mateeteh kolorateh
coloring pencils

BUYING CLOTHES

I am looking for…	Sto cercando… *stoh cherkandoh*
I am size…	Porto la taglia… *portoh lah talya*
Do you have this…	Avete questo/a… *aveteh kwestoh/ah*
…in my size?	…nella mia taglia? *nellah meeah talya*
…in small	…in taglia piccola? *een talya peekolah*
…in medium?	…in taglia media? *een talya medya*
…in large?	…in taglia grande? *een talya grandeh*
…in other colors?	…in altri colori? *een altree koloree*
May I try this on?	Posso provarlo/a? *possoh provarloh/ah*
Where are the changing rooms?	Dove sono gli spogliatoi? *doveh sonoh lye spolyatooee*
It's…	È… *eh*
…too big	…troppo grande *troppoh grandeh*
…too small	…troppo piccolo/a *troppoh peekoloh/ah*
I need…	Ho bisogno di… *oh beezonyo dee*
…a larger size	…una taglia più grande *oonah talya pew grandeh*
…a smaller size	…una taglia più piccola *oonah talya pew peekolah*
I'll take this one, please	Prendo questo/a, grazie *prendoh kwestoh/ah gratsye*
Is this on sale?	È in saldo? *eh een saldoh*

BUYING SHOES

I take shoe size…	Mi serve un… *mee serveh oon*
May I try…	Posso provare… *possoh provareh*
…this pair?	…questo paio? *kwestoh payo*
…those in the window?	…quelle in vetrina? *kwelleh een vetreenah*
These are…	Queste sono… *kwesteh sonoh*
…too tight	…troppo strette *troppoh stretteh*
…too big	…troppo larghe *troppoh largeh*
…too small	…troppo piccole *troppoh peekoleh*
…uncomfortable	…scomode *skomodeh*
Is there a bigger/ smaller size?	Avete un numero più grande/piccolo? *aveteh oon noomeroh pew grandeh/peekoloh*

Clothes and shoe sizes guide

Women's clothes sizes

UK	6	8	10	12	14	16	18	20
Europe	34	36	38	40	42	44	46	48
US	4	6	8	10	12	14	16	18

Men's clothes sizes

UK	36	38	40	42	44	46	48	50
Europe	46	48	50	52	54	56	58	60
US	36	38	40	42	44	46	48	50

Women's shoes

UK	3	4	5	6	7	8	9
Europe	36	37	38	39	40	42	43
US	5	6	7	8	9	10	11

CLOTHES AND SHOES

il vestito
eel vesteetoh
dress

l'abito da sera
labeetoh dah serah
evening dress

la giacca
lah jakkah
jacket

il maglione
eel malyoneh
sweater

i jeans
ee jeenz
jeans

la gonna
lah gonnah
skirt

la scarpa da ginnastica
lah skarpah dah jeennasteekah
sneaker

lo stivale
loh steevaleh
boot

la borsa
lah borzah
handbag

la cintura
lah cheentoorah
belt

il vestito da uomo
eel vesteetoh dah womoh
suit

il cappotto
eel kapottoh
coat

la camicia
lah kameechya
shirt

la T-shirt
lah t-shirt
T-shirt

i calzoncini
ee kaltsoncheenee
shorts

la scarpa col tacco alto
lah skarpah kol takko altoh
high-heeled shoe

la scarpa con lacci
lah skarpah kon latchee
lace-up shoe

il sandalo
eel sandaloh
sandal

l'infradito
leenfradeetoh
flip-flop

i calzini
ee kalseenee
socks

AT THE GIFT SHOP

I'd like to buy a gift for...	Vorrei acquistare un regalo per... *vorray akweestareh oon regaloh pehr*
...my mother/father	...mia madre/mio padre *meeah madreh/meeoh padreh*
...my daughter/son	...mia figlia/mio figlio *meeah feelya/meeoh feelyo*
...a child	...un/a bambino/a *oon/ah bambeenoh/ah*
...a friend	...un/a amico/a *oon/ah ameekoh/ah*
Can you recommend something?	Mi può consigliare qualcosa? *mee pwo konseelyareh kwalkosah*
Do you have a box for it?	Ha la scatola? *ah lah skatolah*
Can you gift wrap it?	Può fare un pacchetto regalo? *pwo fareh oon pakettoh regaloh*

la collana
lah kollanah
necklace

il bracciale
eel bratchyaleh
bracelet

l'orologio
lorolojoh
watch

i gemelli
ee jemellee
cuff links

la bambola
lah bambolah
doll

il peluche
eel peloosh
stuffed animal

il portafoglio
eel portafolyo
wallet

i cioccolatini
ee chokolateenee
chocolates

I want a souvenir of…	Desidero un souvenir di… *deseederoh oon soovenir dee*
Do you have anything cheaper?	Ha qualcosa di meno caro? *ah kwalkosah dee menoh karoh*
Is there a guarantee?	È coperto/a da garanzia? *eh kopertoh/ah dah garantsya*

You may hear...

- **È un regalo?**
  eh oon regaloh
  Is it a present?

- **Vuole un pacchetto regalo?**
  vwoleh oon pakettoh regaloh
  Shall I gift wrap it?

PHOTOGRAPHY

I'd like this film developed	Vorrei sviluppare questa pellicola *vorray sveeloopareh kwestah pelleekolah*
Do you have an express service?	Avete un servizio espresso? *aveteh oon serveetsyo espressoh*
Does it cost more?	Costa di più? *kostah dee pew*
I'd like...	Vorrei... *vorray*
...the one-hour service	...lo sviluppo in un'ora *loh sveeloopoh een oonorah*
...a battery	...una batteria *oonah battereeya*

la fotocamera digitale
lah fotokamerah deejeetaleh
digital camera

la scheda di memoria
lah skedah dee memorya
memory card

il rullino
eel rooleenoh
roll of film

l'album delle fotografie
lalboom delleh fotografye
photo album

la cornice
lah korneeche
photo frame

Do you print digital photos?	Stampate le fotografie digitali? *stampateh leh fotografye deejeetalee*
Can you print from this memory stick?	Potete stampare da questa chiavetta USB? *poteteh stampareh dah kwestah kyakettah oo-es-bee*

il flash
eel flash
flash gun

la fotocamera
lah fotokamerah
camera

gli obiettivi
lyee obyeteevee
lens

la borsa per fotocamera
lah borsah pehr fotokamerah
camera bag

You may hear...

- **Quale formato di foto desidera?**
  kwaleh formatoh deseedeerah
  What size prints do you want?

- **Opache o lucide?**
  opakeh oh loocheedeh?
  Matte or gloss?

AT THE POST OFFICE

I'd like…	Vorrei… *vorray*
…three stamps, please	…tre francobolli, per favore *treh frankobollee pehr favoreh*
…to send a registered letter	…inviare una raccomandata *eenvyareh oonah rakomandatah*
…to send this airmail	…inviare questo per posta aerea *eenvyareh kwestoh pehr postah ahehreha*

la busta
lah boostah
envelope

i francobolli
ee frankobollee
stamps

la cartolina
lah kartoleenah
postcard

la posta aerea
lah postah ahehreha
airmail

You may hear…

- **Cosa contiene?**
  kozah kontyeneh
  What are the contents?

- **Qual è il suo valore?**
  kwaleh eel soo-oh valoreh
  What is their value?

- **Riempia questo modulo.**
  ryempya kwestoh modooloh
  Fill out this form.

How much is...?	Quanto costa... *kwantoh kostah*
...a letter to...	...una lettera per... *oonah letterah pehr*
...a postcard to...	...una cartolina per... *oonah kartoleenah pehr*
...the United States	...gli Stati Uniti *lyee statee oonectee*

il pacco
eel pakoh
package

il corriere
eel korryereh
courier

la cassetta delle lettere
lah kassettah delleh lettereh
mailbox

il postino
eel posteenoh
mail carrier

...Great Britain	...la Gran Bretagna *lah gran bretanya*
...Canada	...il Canada *eel kanadah*
...Australia	...l'Australia *lowstralya*
May I have a receipt?	Posso avere la ricevuta? *possoh avereh lah reechevootah*
Where can I mail this?	Dove posso imbucare questa lettera? *doveh possoh eembookareh kwestah letterah*

TELEPHONES

Where is the nearest phone booth?

Dov'è la cabina telefonica più vicina?
doveh lah kabeenah telefoneekah pew veecheenah

il telefono
eel telefonoh
phone

il cellulare
eel chelloolareh
cell phone

la scheda telefonica
lah skedah telefoneekah
phone card

la cabina telefonica
lah kabeenah telefoneekah
telephone booth

il telefono a moneta
eel telefonoh ah monetah
pay phone

la segreteria telefonica
lah segreterya telefoneekah
answering machine

Who's speaking?	Pronto, chi parla? *prontoh kee parlah*
Hello, this is…	Pronto, sono… *prontoh sonoh*
I'd like to speak with…	Vorrei parlare con… *vorray parlareh kon*

INTERNET

Is there an internet café near here?	C'è un Internet cafè qui vicino? *che oon eenternet kafeh kwee veecheenoh*
How much do you charge?	Quanto costa? *kwantoh kostah*
Do you have wireless internet?	Avete un sistema Internet wireless? *aveteh oon seestemah eenternet wireless*
Can I check my emails?	Posso controllare le mie e-mail? *possoh kontrollareh leh meeyeh emayl*
I need to send an email	Devo inviare un'e-mail *devoh eenvyareh oonemayl*
What's your email address?	Qual è il suo indirizzo e-mail? *kwaleh eel soo-oh eendeereedzo emayl*
My email address is...	Il mio indirizzo e-mail è... *eel meeoh eendeereedzo emayl eh*

il computer portatile
eel compewter portateeleh
laptop

la tastiera
lah tastyerah
keyboard

il sito Web
eel seetoh web
website

l'e-mail
lemayl
email

SIGHTSEEING

Most Italian cities and towns have a tourist information office, which is usually situated near the railroad station or town hall. The staff will advise you on local places of interest to visit. In Italy, most national museums close on Mondays as well as on public holidays, so make sure that you check the opening times before visiting.

AT THE TOURIST OFFICE

Where is the tourist information office?	Dov'è l'ufficio del turismo? *doveh loofeechyo del tooreesmoh*
Can you recommend...	Può consigliarmi... *pwo konseelyarmee*
...a guided tour?	...una visita guidata? *oonah veeseetah gweedatah*
...an excursion?	...una gita? *oonah jeetah*
Is there a museum or art gallery?	C'è un museo o una galleria d'arte? *che oon moozeoh oh oonah gallereeya darteh*
Is it open to the public?	È aperto/a al pubblico? *eh apertoh/ah al poobleekoh*
Is there wheelchair access?	C'è un accesso per disabili? *che oon atchessoh pehr deezabeelee*
Does it close...	È chiuso/a... *eh kewsoh/ah*
...on Sundays?	...la domenica? *lah domeneekah*
...on public holidays?	...nei giorni festivi? *nay jornee festeevee*
How long does it take to get there?	Quanto ci vuole per arrivarci? *kwantoh chee vwoleh pehr areevarchee*
Do you have...	Avete... *aveteh*
...a street map?	...una cartina? *oonah karteenah*
...a guide?	...una guida? *oonah gweedah*
...any leaflets?	...degli opuscoli? *dehlyee opooskolee*

VISITING PLACES

What time…	A che ora… *ah ke orah*
…do you open?	…apre? *apreh*
…do you close?	…chiude? *kewdeh*
I'd like two entrance tickets	Vorrei due biglietti d'entrata *vorray dooeh beelyettee dentratah*
Two adults, please	Due adulti, per favore *dooeh adooltee pehr favoreh*
A family ticket	Un biglietto famiglia *oon beelyettoh fameelya*
How much does it cost?	Quanto costa? *kwantoh kostah*
Are there reductions for…	Ci sono delle riduzioni per… *chee sonoh delleh reedootsyonee pehr*
…children?	…i bambini? *ee bambeenee*
…students?	…gli studenti? *lyee stoodentee*

la pianta della città
lah pyantah dellah cheetah
street map

l'ufficio del turismo
loofeechyo del tooreesmoh
tourist office

il biglietto d'entrata
eel beelyettoh dentratah
entrance ticket

l'accesso disabili
latchessoh deezabeelee
wheelchair access

Can I buy a guidebook?	Posso acquistare una guida? *possoh akweestareh oonah gweedah*
Is there...	C'è... *che*
...an audio guide?	...un'audio guida? *oonowdyo gweedah*
...a guided tour?	...una visita guidata? *oonah veeseetah gweedatah*
...an elevator?	...un ascensore? *oon ashenzoreh*
...a bus tour?	...un giro turistico in autobus? *oon jeeroh tooreesteeko een owtoboos*
When is the next tour?	Quando parte il prossimo giro turistico? *kwandoh parteh eel proseemoh jeeroh tooreesteeko*

il tour in autobus
eel tour een owtoboos
tour bus

You may hear...

- **Possiede una carta studenti?**
  possyedeh oonah kartah stoodentee
  Do you have a student card?

- **Quanti anni ha?**
  kwantee annee ah
  How old are you?

FINDING YOUR WAY

Excuse me	Mi scusi *mee skoozee*
Can you help me?	Mi può aiutare? *mee pwo ayewtareh*
Is this the way to...?	È questa la strada per...? *eh kwestah lah stradah pehr*
How do I get to...?	Come raggiungo...? *komeh rajewngoh*
...the town center?	...il centro della città? *eel chentroh dellah cheetah*
...the station?	...la stazione? *lah statsyoneh*
...the museum?	...il museo? *eel moozeoh*
...the art gallery?	...la galleria d'arte? *lah gallereeya darteh*
How long does it take?	Quanto tempo s'impiega? *kwantoh tempoh seempyegah*
Is it far?	È lontano? *eh lontanoh*
Can you show me on the map?	Me lo può indicare sulla cartina? *meh loh pwo eendeekareh soolah karteenah*

You may hear...

- **Non è lontano.**
  non eh lontanoh
  It's not far away.

- **Ci vogliono dieci minuti.**
  chee volyonoh deeaychee meenootee
  It takes ten minutes.

You may hear...

- **Siamo qui**
  syamoh kwee

  We are here

- **Vada sempre dritto...**
  vadah sempreh dreetoh

  Keep going straight...

- **...fino alla fine della via**
  feenoh allah feeneh dellah veeya

  ...to the end of the street

- **...fino al semaforo**
  feenoh al semaforoh

  ...to the traffic lights

- **...fino alla piazza principale**
  feenoh allah pyadza preencheepaleh

  ...to the main square

- **Di qua**
  dee kwa

  This way

- **Di là**
  dee lah

  That way

- **Svolti a destra al/alla...**
  svoltee ah destrah al/allah

  Turn right at...

- **Svolti a sinistra al/alla...**
  svoltee ah seeneestrah al/allah

  Turn left at...

- **Prenda la prima...**
  prendah lah preemah

  Take the first...

- **...a sinistra/a destra**
  ah seeneestrah/ah destrah

  ...on the left/right

- **È davanti a lei**
  eh davantee ah lay

  It's in front of you

- **È dietro di lei**
  eh deeyehtroh dee lay

  It's behind you

- **È di fronte a lei**
  eh dee fronteh ah lay

  It's opposite you

- **È vicino a...**
  eh veecheenoh ah

  It's next to...

- **C'è un'indicazione**
  che ooneendeekatsyoneh

  It's signposted

- **È là**
  eh lah

  It's over there

PLACES TO VISIT

il municipio
eel mooneecheepyo
town hall

il ponte
eel ponteh
bridge

il museo
eel moozeoh
museum

la galleria d'arte
lah gallereeya darteh
art gallery

il monumento
eel monoomentoh
monument

la chiesa
lah kyezah
church

la cattedrale
lah katedraleh
cathedral

il paese
eel paheseh
village

il parco
eel parkoh
park

il porto
eel portoh
harbor

il faro
eel faroh
lighthouse

il vigneto
eel veenyetoh
vineyard

il castello
eel kastelloh
castle

la costa
lah kostah
coast

la cascata
lah kaskatah
waterfall

le montagne
leh montanye
mountains

OUTDOOR ACTIVITIES

Where can we go…	Dove possiamo… *doveh possyamoh*
…horseback riding?	…andare a cavallo? *andareh ah kavalloh*
…fishing?	…andare a pescare? *andareh ah peskareh*
…swimming?	…nuotare? *nwotareh*
…walking?	…fare un'escursione a piedi? *fareh oon eskoorzyoneh ah pyedee*
Can we…	Possiamo… *possyamoh*
…rent equipment?	…noleggiare l'attrezzatura? *noledjareh lattredzatoorah*
…have lessons?	…prendere delle lezioni? *prendereh delleh letsyonee*
How much per hour?	Quanto costa all'ora? *kwantoh kostah allorah*
I'm a beginner	Sono un/a principiante *sonoh oon/ah preencheepyanteh*
I'm very experienced	Ho una buona esperienza *Oh oonah bwonah esperyentsah*
Where's the amusement park?	Dov'è il parco dei divertimenti? *doveh eel parkoh day deeverteementee*
Can the children go on all the rides?	I bambini possono andare su tutte le giostre? *ee bambeenee possonoh andareh soo tooteh leh jostreh*
Is there a playground?	C'è un'area giochi? *che oon ahrehah jokee*
Is it safe for children?	È sicura per i bambini? *eh seekoorah pehr ee bambeenee*

il luna park
eel loonah park
fairground

il parco a tema
eel parkoh ah temah
theme park

il parco safari
eel parkoh safaree
safari park

lo zoo
loh dzoh
zoo

l'area giochi
larehah jokee
playground

il picnic
eel picnic
picnic

pescare
peskareh
fishing

andare a cavallo
andareh ah kavalloh
horseback riding

SPORTS AND LEISURE

Italy can offer the traveler a wide range of cultural events, entertainments, leisure activities, and sports. The Italians are proud of their rich artistic and musical heritage, and their distinctive culture is very important to them. For the sports enthusiast, a wide range of spectator sports and facilities are available, from winter sports, climbing and hiking in the Alps and Appenine,s to watersports around the coast and on inland lakes. Soccer is the national game and you can watch a *Serie A* match.

LEISURE TIME

I like...	Mi piace/piacciono... *mee pyaceh/pyatchyonoh*
...art and painting	...l'arte e la pittura *larteh eh lah peetoorah*
...movies and cinema	...i film e il cinema *ee film eh eel cheenemah*
...the theater	...il teatro *eel tehatroh*
...opera	...l'opera *loperah*
I prefer...	Preferisco... *prefereeskoh*
...reading books	...leggere libri *ledjereh leebree*
...listening to music	...ascoltare musica *askoltareh moozeekah*
...watching sports	...guardare lo sport *gwardareh loh sport*
...playing games	...giocare a qualcosa *jokareh ah kwalkosah*
...going to concerts	...andare ai concerti *andareh ahee konchertee*
...dancing	...ballare *ballareh*
...going to clubs	...andare in discoteca *andareh een deeskotekah*
...going out with friends	...uscire con gli amici *oosheereh kon lyee ameechee*
I don't like...	Non mi piace... *non mee pyacheh*
That bores me	Mi annoia *mee annoyah*
That doesn't interest me	Non mi interessa *non mee eenteressah*

AT THE BEACH

Can I rent…	Posso noleggiare… *possoh noledjareh*
…a jet ski?	…una moto d'acqua? *oonah motoh dakwa*
…a beach umbrella?	…un ombrellone da mare? *oon ombrelloneh dah mareh*
…a surfboard?	…una tavola da surf? *oonah tavolah dah surf*
…a wetsuit?	…una muta subacquea? *oonah mootah soobakweah*

il telo da mare
eel teloh dah mareh
beach towel

il pallone da spiaggia
eel palloneh dah speeadjah
beach ball

la sedia a sdraio
lah sedya ah sdrayo
deck chair

il lettino sdraio
eel leteenoh sdrayo
lounge chair

You may hear…

- **Divieto di balneazione.**
  deevyetoh dee balneatsyoneh
  No swimming

- **Spiaggia chiusa.**
  speeadja kewsah
  Beach closed

gli occhiali da sole
lyee okccalee dalı soleh
sunglasses

il cappello da sole
eel kappeloh dah soleh
sun hat

il bikini
eel beekeenee
bikini

la lozione solare
lah lotsyoneh solareh
suntan lotion

le pinne
leh peenneh
flippers

la maschera e il boccaglio
lah maskerah eh eel bokalyo
mask and snorkel

How much does it cost?	Quanto costa? *kwantoh kostah*
Can I go water-skiing?	Posso fare dello sci d'acqua? *possoh fareh delloh shee dakwa*
Is there a lifeguard?	C'è il bagnino? *che eel baneenoh*
Is it safe to…	È sicuro… *eh seekooroh*
…swim here?	…nuotare qui? *nwotareh kwee*
…surf here?	…fare del surf qui? *fareh del surf kwee*

AT THE SWIMMING POOL

What time...	Quando... *kwandoh*
...does the pool open?	...apre la piscina? *apreh lah peesheenah*
...does the pool close?	...chiude la piscina? *kewdeh lah peesheenah*
Is it...	È... *eh*
...an indoor pool?	...una piscina coperta? *oonah peesheenah kopertah*
...an outdoor pool?	...una piscina all'aperto? *oonah peesheenah alapertoh*
Is there a children's pool?	C'è una piscina per bambini? *che oonah peesheenah pehr bambeenee*
Where are the changing rooms?	Dove sono gli spogliatoi? *doveh sonoh lyee spolyatoy*
Is it safe to dive?	È sicuro tuffarsi? *eh seekooroh toofarsee*

i braccioli
ee bratchyolee
armband

la tavoletta
lah tavolettah
float

gli occhialini
lyee okyaleenee
swimming goggles

il costume
eel kostoomeh
swimsuit

AT THE GYM

il vogatore
eel vogatoreh
rowing machine

l'ellittica
lelleeteekah
cross trainer

la step machine
lah step machine
step machine

la bicicletta
lah beecheeklettah
exercise bike

Is there a gym?	C'è una palestra? *che oonah palestrah*
Is it free for guests?	È gratuita per i clienti? *eh gratooeetah pehr ee klyentee*
Do I have to wear sneakers?	Devo indossare le scarpe da ginnastica? *devoh eendossareh leh skarpeh dah jeennasteekah*
Do I need an introductory session?	Devo fare una sessione introduttiva? *devoh fareh oonah sessyoneh introdootteevah*
Do you offer...	Offrite... *offreeteh*
...aerobics classes?	...lezioni di aerobica? *letsyonee dee aerobeekah*
...Pilates classes?	...lezioni di Pilates? *letsyonee dee pilates*
...yoga classes?	...lezioni di yoga? *letsyonee dee yogah*

BOATING AND SAILING

Can I rent...	Posso noleggiare... *possoh noledjareh*
...a dinghy?	...un gommone? *oon gommoneh*
...a windsurf board?	...una tavola da windsurf? *oonah tavolah dah windsurf*
...a canoe?	...una canoa? *oonah kanoah*

il giubbotto di salvataggio
eel jewbottoh dee salvatadjoh
life jacket

la bussola
lah boosolah
compass

Do you offer sailing lessons?	Offrite lezioni di vela? *offreeteh letsyonee dee velah*
Do you have a mooring?	Avete un ormeggio? *aveteh oon ormedjoh*
How much is it for the night?	Quanto costa per notte? *kwantoh kostah pehr notteh*
Where can I buy gas?	Dove posso comprare del gas? *doveh possoh komprahray del gaz?*
Where is the marina?	Dov'è il porticciolo? *doveh eel porteetchyoloh*
My...is broken	Il mio/la mia...non funziona *eel meeoh/lah meeah... non foontsyonah*
Can you repair it?	Potete ripararlo/a? *poteteh reepararloh/ah*
Are there life jackets?	Ci sono dei giubbotti di salvataggio? *chee sonoh day jewbottee dee salvatadjoh*

WINTER SPORTS

I would like to rent...	Desidero noleggiare... *deseederoh noledjareh*
...some skis	...un paio di sci *oon payo dee shee*
...some ski boots	...un paio di scarponi *oon payo dee skarponee*
...some poles	...un paio di racchette *oon payo dee raketteh*
...a snowboard	...uno snowboard *oonoh snowboard*
...a helmet	...un casco *oon kaskoh*
When does...	Quando... *kwandoh*
...the chair lift open?	...apre la seggiovia? *apreh lah sedjoveeya*
...the cable car close?	...chiude la funivia? *kewdeh lah fooneeveeya*
How much is a lift pass?	Quanto costa un pass? *kwantoh kostah oon pass*
Can I take skiing lessons?	Posso prendere delle lezioni di sci? *possoh prendereh delleh letsyonee dee shee*

You may hear...

• È un principiante?
 eh oon preencheepeeanteh
 Are you a beginner?

• Deve lasciare un deposito.
 deveh lashyareh oon deposeetoh
 I need a deposit.

BALL GAMES

I like playing…	Mi piace giocare a… *mee pyacheh jokareh ah*
…soccer	…pallone *palloneh*
…tennis	…tennis *tennis*
…golf	…golf *golf*
…badminton	…volano *volahnoh*
…squash	…squash *skwosh*
…baseball	…baseball *besboll*
Where is the nearest…	Dov'è il più vicino… *doveh eel pew veecheenoh*
…tennis court?	…campo da tennis? *kampoh dah tennis*
…golf course?	…campo da golf? *kampoh dah golf*
…sports center?	…centro sportivo? *chentroh sporteevoh*

il pallone
eel palloneh
soccer ball

i polsini
ee polseenee
wristbands

il canestro
eel kanestroh
basketball hoop

il guanto da baseball
eel gwantoh dah besball
baseball glove

May I book a court...	Posso prenotare un campo... *possoh prenotareh oon kampoh*
...for two hours?	...per due ore? *pehr dooeh oreh*
...at three o'clock?	...per le tre? *pehr leh tray*
What shoes are allowed?	Quali scarpe sono permesse? *kwalee skarpeh sonoh permesseh*
May I rent...	Posso noleggiare... *possoh noledjareh*
...a tennis racket?	...una racchetta da tennis? *oonah rakettah dah tennis*
...some balls?	...delle palle? *delleh palleh*
...a set of clubs?	...un set di mazze? *oon set dee madze*
...a golf cart?	...il carrello elettrico? *eel karreloh elettreekoh*

la racchetta
lah rakettah
tennis racket

le palle
leh palleh
tennis balls

la palla e il tee
lah pallah eh eel tee
golf ball and tee

la mazza
lah madza
golf club

GOING OUT

Where is...	Dov'è... *doveh*
...the opera house?	...il teatro dell'opera? *eel teatroh delloperah*
...a jazz club?	...il jazz club? *eel jazz clab*
Do I have to book in advance?	Devo prenotare in anticipo? *devoh prenotareh een anteecheepoh*
I'd like...tickets	Vorrei...biglietti *vorray...beelyettee*
I'd like seats...	Vorrei dei posti... *vorray day postee*
...in the back	...in fondo *een fondoh*
...in the front	...davanti *davantee*
...in the middle	...nel mezzo *nel medzo*
...in the gallery	...in galleria *een gallereeya*
Can I buy a program?	Posso acquistare un programma? *possoh akweestareh oon programmah*
Is there live music?	C'è musica dal vivo? *che moozeekah dal veevoh*

You may hear...

- **Spenga il cellulare.**
  spengah eel chelloolareh
  Turn off your cell phone.

- **Torni a sedere.**
  tornee ah sedereh
  Return to your seats.

il teatro
eel teatroh
theater

il teatro dell'opera
eel teatroh delloperah
opera house

il musicista
eel moozeecheestah
musician

il pianista
eel pyaneestah
pianist

il/la cantante
eel/lah kantanteh
singer

la danza
lah dandza
ballet

il cinema
eel cheenemah
movie theater

i popcorn
ee popcorn
popcorn

il casinò
eel kaseenoh
casino

il nightclub
eel naitklab
nightclub

GALLERIES AND MUSEUMS

What are the opening hours?	Qual è l'oraryo di apertura? *kwaleh loraryo dapertoorah*
Are there guided tours in English?	Ci sono delle visite guidate in inglese? *chee sonoh delleh veezeeteh gweedateh een eengleseh*
When does the tour leave?	Quando inizia la visita? *kwandoh eeneetsya lah veeseetah*
How much does it cost?	Quanto costa? *kwantoh kostah*
How long does it take?	Quanto dura? *kwantoh doorah*
Do you have an audio guide?	Avete delle guide audio? *aveteh delleh gweedeh owdyo*
Do you have a guidebook in English?	Avete una guida in inglese? *aveteh oonah gweedah een eengleseh*
Can you direct me to…?	Mi può indirizzare a…? *mee pwo eendeereetsareh ah*
Is (flash) photography allowed?	Sono permesse le fotografie (con il flash)? *sonoh permesseh leh fotografye (kon eel flash)*

la statua
lah statwa
statue

il busto
eel boostoh
bust

I'd really like to see…	Mi piacerebbe molto visitare… *mee pyacherebbeh moltoh veezeetareh*
Who painted this?	Chi è l'autore di questo quadro? *ki eh lowtoreh dee kwostoh kwadroh*
How old is it?	A quando risale? *ah kwandoh reesaleh*

il dipinto
eel deepeentoh
painting

l'incisione
leencheesyoneh
engraving

il disegno
eel deesenyo
drawing

il manoscritto
eel manoskreettoh
manuscript

Are there wheelchair ramps?	Ci sono delle rampe per disabili? *chee sonoh delleh rampeh pehr deezabeelee*
Is there an elevator?	C'è un ascensore? *che oon ashenzoreh*
Where are the restrooms?	Dov'è la toilette? *doveh lah twalet*
I've lost my group	Ho perso il mio gruppo *oh persoh eel meeoh grooppoh*

HOME ENTERTAINMENT

How do I...	Come... *komeh*
...turn the television on?	...accendo il televisore? *atchendoh eel televeezoreh*
...change channels?	...cambio i canali? *kambyo ee kanalee*
...turn the volume up?	...alzo il volume? *altso eel voloomeh*
...turn the volume down?	...abbasso il volume? *abassoh eel voloomeh*
Do you have satellite TV?	Avete una TV satellitare? *aveteh oonah TV satelleetareh*
Where can I buy...	Dove posso acquistare... *doveh possoh akweestareh*
...a DVD?	...un DVD? *oon deeveedee*
...a music CD?	...un CD musicale? *oon cheedee moozeekaleh*
...an audio CD?	...un CD audio? *oon cheedee owdyo*

il televisore a schermo panoramico
eel televeezoreh ah skermoh panorameekoh
widescreen TV

il lettore DVD
eel lettoreh deeveedee
DVD player

il telecomando
eel telekomandoh
remote control

il videogioco
eel videojokoh
video game

il lettore CD
eel lettoreh cheedee
CD player

l'iPod
lipod
iPod

la radio
lah radyo
radio

il portatile
eel portateeleh
laptop

il mouse
eel mows
mouse

Can I use this to…	Posso usarlo per… *possoh oozarloh pehr*
…go online?	…accedere ad Internet? *atchedereh ad eenternet*
Is it broadband/wifi?	È a banda larga/wifi? *eh ah bandah largah/wifi*
How do I…	Come… *komeh*
…log on?	…mi connetto? *mee konnettoh*
…log out?	…mi disconetto? *mee deeskonnettoh*
…reboot?	…riavvio il computer? *reeyaveeyo eel compooter*

HEALTH

A European Health Insurance Card entitles EU nationals to free emergency medical treatment in Italy. Citizens of other countries should have travel insurance or check that their domestic insurer covers them abroad. It is wise to familiarize yourself with a few phrases for use in an emergency, or if you need to visit a pharmacy, doctor, dentist, or hospital.

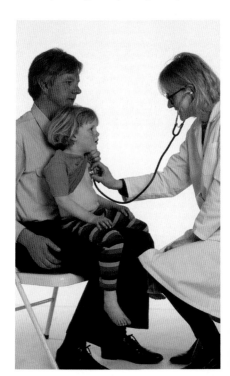

USEFUL PHRASES

I need a doctor	Ho bisogno di un medico *oh beezonyo dee oon medeekoh*
I would like an appointment...	Vorrei prendere un appuntamento... *vorray prendereh oon apoontamentoh*
...as soon as possible	...al più presto possibile *al pew prestoh posseebeeleh*
...today	...per oggi *pehr ojee*
...tomorrow	...per domani *pehr domanee*
It's very urgent	È molto urgente *eh moltoh oorjenteh*
I have a European Health Insurance Card	Possiedo una carta di assistenza sanitaria europea *possyedoh oonah kartah dee asseestentsa saneetarya ehooropayah*
I have health insurance	Ho un'assicurazione sanitaria *oh oon asseekooratsyoneh saneetarya*
May I have a receipt?	Posso avere la ricevuta? *possoh avereh lah reechevootah*
Where is the nearest...	Dov'è il più vicino/a... *doveh eel pew veecheenoh/ah*
...pharmacy?	...farmacia? *farmacheeya*
...doctor's office?	...ambulatorio medico? *amboolatoryo medeekoh*
...hospital?	...ospedale? *ospedaleh*
...dentist?	...dentista? *denteestah*

AT THE PHARMACY

What can I take for...?	Cosa posso prendere per...? *kozah possoh prendereh* *pehr*
How many should I take?	Quante ne devo prendere? *kwanteh neh devoh* *prendereh*
Is it safe for children?	È sicuro/a per i bambini? *eh seekooroh/ah pehr ee* *bambeenee*
Are there side effects?	Ha degli effetti indesiderati? *ah delyee effetee* *eendeseederatee*
Do you have that...	Questo prodotto viene venduto... *kwestoh prodottoh vyeneh* *vendootoh*
...as tablets?	...in compresse? *een kompresseh*
...in capsule form?	...in capsule? *een kapsooleh*
I'm allergic to...	Sono allergico/a a... *sonoh allerjeekoh/ah ah*
I'm already taking...	Sto già prendendo... *stoh jah prendendoh*
Do I need a prescription?	Ho bisogno della ricetta medica? *oh beezonyo dellah* *reechettah medeekah*

You may hear...

- **Prenda questo/a...**
  volte al giorno.
  prendah kwestoh/ah...
  volteh al jornoh
  Take this...times a day.

- **Durante i pasti.**
  dooranteh ee pastee
  With food.

le bende
leh bendeh
bandage

il cerotto
eel cherottoh
adhesive bandage

le capsule
leh kapsooleh
capsules

le compresse
leh compresseh
pills

l'inalatore
leenalatoreh
inhaler

le supposte
leh soopposteh
suppositories

le gocce
leh goccheh
drops

lo spray
loh spry
spray

la pomata
lah pomatah
ointment

lo sciroppo
loh sheeroppoh
syrup

THE HUMAN BODY

I have hurt my…

Mi sono fatto/a male
al/alla…
*mee sonoh fattoh/ah
maleh al/allah*

il gomito
eel gomeetoh
elbow

la spalla
lah spallah
shoulder

il torace
eel torache
chest

la gamba
lah gambah
leg

il braccio
eel bratchyo
arm

la testa
lah testah
head

il collo
eel kolloh
neck

lo stomaco
loh stomakoh
stomach

il ginocchio
eel jeenokyo
knee

il piede
eel pyedeh
foot

FACE

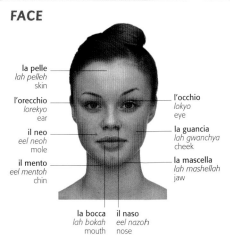

la pelle
lah pelleh
skin

l'orecchio
lorekyo
ear

il neo
eel neoh
mole

il mento
eel mentoh
chin

l'occhio
lokyo
eye

la guancia
lah gwanchya
cheek

la mascella
lah mashellah
jaw

la bocca
lah bokah
mouth

il naso
eel nazoh
nose

HAND   FOOT

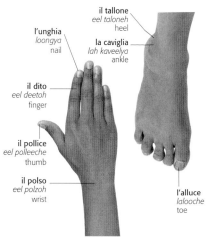

il tallone
eel taloneh
heel

la caviglia
lah kaveelya
ankle

l'unghia
loongya
nail

il dito
eel deetoh
finger

il pollice
eel polleeche
thumb

il polso
eel polzoh
wrist

l'alluce
lalooche
toe

FEELING SICK

I don't feel well	Non mi sento bene
	non mee sentoh beneh
I feel sick	Mi sento male
	mee sentoh maleh
I have...	Ho...
	Oh
...an ear ache	...mal d'orecchio
	mal dorekyo
...a stomach ache	...mal di stomaco
	mal dee stomakoh
...a sore throat	...la gola infiammata
	lah golah enfyammatah
...a temperature	...la febbre
	lah febbreh
...hayfever	...il raffreddore da fieno
	eel rafreddoreh dah fyenoh
...constipation	...costipazione
	kosteepatsyoneh
...diarrhea	...diarrea
	dyareah
...a toothache	...mal di denti
	mal dee dentee
I've been stung by...	Mi ha punto...
	mee ah poontoh
...a bee/wasp	...un'ape/una vespa
	oonapeh/oonah vespah
...a jellyfish	...una medusa
	oonah medoosah
I've been bitten by...	Mi ha morso...
	mee ah morsoh
...a snake	...un serpente
	oon serpenteh
...a dog	...un cane
	oon kaneh

INJURIES

il taglio
eel talyo
cut

l'escoriazione
leskoryatsyoneh
graze

l'ematoma
lematomah
bruise

la scheggia
lah skedjah
splinter

la scottatura solare
lah skotatoorah solareh
sunburn

la bruciatura
lah broochyatoorah
burn

il morso
eel morsoh
bite

la puntura
lah poontoorah
sting

la distorsione
lah deestorsyoneh
sprain

la frattura
lah fratoorah
fracture

AT THE DOCTOR

I'm...	Sto...
	stoh
...vomiting	...vomitando
	vomeetandoh
...bleeding	...perdendo sangue
	perdendoh sangwe
...dizzy	...ho le vertigini
	oh leh verteejeenee
...feeling faint	...mi sento svenire
	mee sentoh sveneereh
...pregnant	...sono incinta
	sonoh eencheentah
...diabetic	...ho il diabete
	oh eel dyabeteh
...epileptic	...sono epilettico/a
	sonoh epeeletteekoh/ah
I have...	Soffro di...
	soffroh dee
...arthritis	...artrite
	artreeteh
...a heart condition	...una patologia cardiaca
	oonah patolojeea kardeeakah
...high blood pressure	...elevata pressione sanguigna
	elevatah pressyoneh sangweenya

You may hear...

- Cosa c'è che non va?
  kozah che ke non vah
  What's wrong?

- Dove le fa male?
  doveh leh fah maleh
  Where does it hurt?

- Posso visitarla?
  possoh veezeetarlah
  May I examine you?

ILLNESS

il mal di testa
eel mal dee testah
headache

il sangue dal naso
eel sangwe dal nasoh
nosebleed

la tosse
lah tosseh
cough

lo starnuto
loh starnootoh
sneeze

il raffreddore
eel rafreddoreh
cold

l'influenza
leenflooentsa
flu

l'asma
lasmah
asthma

i crampi
ee krampee
stomach cramps

la nausea
lah nowzeah
nausea

l'eruzione cutanea
lerootsyoneh kootaneah
rash

AT THE HOSPITAL

Can you help me?	Mi può aiutare? *mee pwo ayewtareh*
I need...	Ho bisogno di... *oh beezonyo dee*
...a doctor	...un dottore *oon dottoreh*
...a nurse	...un'infermiera *oon eenfermyerah*
Where is...	Dov'è... *doveh*
...the emergency room?	...il Pronto Soccorso? *eel prontoh sokorzoh*
...the children's ward?	...il reparto pediatrico? *eel repartoh pedyatreeko*
...the X-ray department?	...il reparto di radiologia? *eel repartoh dee radyolojah*
...the elevator/stairs?	...l'ascensore/la scala? *lashensoreh/lah skalah*
...the waiting room?	...la sala d'attesa? *lah salah dattesah*

l'iniezione
leenyetsyoneh
injection

le analisi del sangue
leh analeezee del sangwe
blood test

la radiografia
lah radyografya
X-ray

l'ecografia, la TAC
lekografya lah tac
scan

...the intensive care unit?	...il reparto di terapia intensiva? *eel repartoh dee terapya eentenzeevah*
I think I've broken...	Penso di essermi rotto/a... *pensoh dee essermee rottoh/ah*
Do I need...	Ho bisogno di... *oh beezonyo dee*
...an injection?	...un'iniezione? *ooneenyetsyoneh*
...an operation?	...un'operazione? *oonoperatsyoneh*
Will it hurt?	Sarà doloroso/a? *sarah dolorosoh/ah*
How long will it take?	Quanto tempo sarà necessario? *kwantoh tempoh sarah nechessaryo*
What are the visiting hours?	Quali sono gli orari di visita? *kwalee sonoh lyee oraree dee veeseetah*

la sedia a rotelle
lah sedya ah rotelleh
wheelchair

la rianimazione
lah reeaneematsyoneh
resuscitation

la stecca
lah stekkah
splint

la fasciatura
lah fashyatoorah
dressing

EMERGENCIES

In an emergency, you should dial 112 and ask for either an ambulance (*un ambulanza*), the fire department (*i vigili del fuoco*), the police (*la Polizia*), or the military police (*i Carabinieri*), which is part of the army. If you are the victim of a crime or lose your passport and money, you should report the incident to the police. In the following pages, you will find some useful phrases to help you.

IN AN EMERGENCY

Help!	Aiuto! *ayewtoh*
Please go away!	Mi lasci stare! *mee lashee stareh*
Let go!	Lasci! *lashee*
Stop! Thief!	Fermo! Al ladro! *fermoh al ladroh*
Call the police!	Chiamate la polizia! *kiamateh lah poleetseeya*
Get a doctor!	Trovate un dottore! *trovateh oon dottoreh*
I need...	Ho bisogno... *oh beezonyo*
...the police	...della polizia *dellah poleetseeya*
...the fire department	...dei vigili del fuoco *day veejeelee del fwoko*
...an ambulance	...di un'ambulanza *dee oon amboolantsa*
It's very urgent	È molto urgente *eh moltoh oorjenteh*
Where is...	Dov'è... *doveh*
...the American embassy?	...l'ambasciata americana? *lambashyatah amereekanah*
...the American consulate?	...il consolato americano? *eel konsolahtoh amereekanoh*
...the police station?	...il commissariato? *eel komeesareeyatoh*
...the hospital?	...l'ospedale? *lospedaleh*

ACCIDENTS

I need to make a telephone call	Devo fare una telefonata *devoh fareh oonah telefonatah*
I'd like to report an accident	Vorrei denunciare un incidente *vorray denoonchyareh oon eencheedenteh*
I've crashed my car	Ho avuto un incidente d'auto *oh avootoh oon eencheedenteh dowtoh*
The registration number is…	Il numero di targa è… *eel noomeroh dee targah eh*
I'm at…	Mi trovo a/in… *mee trovoh ah/een*
Please come quickly!	Venite subito, per favore! *veneeteh soobeetoh pehr favoreh*
Someone's injured	Qualcuno è ferito *kwalkoonoh eh fereetoh*
Someone's been knocked down	Qualcuno è stato investito *kwalkoonoh eh statoh eenvesteetoh*
There's a fire at…	C'è un incendio a/in… *che oon eenchendyo ah/een*

You may hear...

- Di quale servizio ha bisogno?
  dee kwaleh serveetsyo ah beezonyo
  Which service do you require?

- Cos'è successo?
  kozeh sootchessoh
  What happened?

EMERGENCY SERVICES

l'ambulanza
lamboolantsa
ambulance

i vigili del fuoco
ee veejeelee del fwoko
firefighters

l'autopompa
lowtopompah
fire engine

l'allarme antincendio
lalarmeh anteenchendyo
fire alarm

l'idrante
leedranteh
hydrant

l'estintore
lesteentoreh
fire extinguisher

le manette
leh manetteh
handcuffs

la volante
lah volanteh
police car

il poliziotto
eel poleetsyottoh
policeman

POLICE AND CRIME

I want to report a crime	Desidero sporgere denuncia *deseederoh sporjereh denoonchya*
I've been...	Sono vittima... *sonoh veeteemah*
...robbed	...di un furto *dee oon foortoh*
...attacked	...di un attacco *dee oon attakko*
...mugged	...di un borseggio *dee oon borsejoh*
...raped	...di una violenza sessuale *dee oonah vyolentsa sessooaleh*
...burgled	...di un furto *dee oon foortoh*
Someone has stolen...	Qualcuno ha rubato... *kwalkoonoh ah roobatoh*
...my car	...la mia auto *lah meeah owtoh*
...my money	...il mio denaro *eel meeoh denaroh*
...my traveler's checks	...i miei traveller's cheques *ee myeh-ee traveller's cheques*
...my passport	...il mio passaporto *eel meeoh passaportoh*

You may hear...

- **Quando è successo?**
  kwandoh eh sootchessoh
  When did it happen?

- **Ci sono testimoni?**
  chee sonoh testeemonee
  Was there a witness?

- **Si ricorda l'aspetto?**
  see reekordah laspettoh
  What did he look like?

I'd like to speak to…	Vorrei parlare con… *vorray parlareh kon*
…a senior officer	…un responsabile *oon responsabeeleh*
…a policewoman	…una poliziotta *oonah poleetsyottah*
I need…	Ho bisogno di… *oh beezonyo dee*
…a lawyer	…un avvocato *oon avokatoh*
…an interpreter	…un interprete *oon eenterpreteh*
…to make a phone call	…fare una telefonata *fareh oonah telefonatah*
I'm very sorry, officer	Mi spiace molto, signor agente *mee spyacheh moltoh seenyor ajenteh*
Here is…	Ecco… *ekko*
…my driver's license	…la patente *lah patenteh*
…my insurance	…l'assicurazione *lasseekooratsyoneh*
How much is the fine?	A quanto ammonta la multa? *ah kwantoh ammontah lah mooltah*

You may hear…

- Favorisca la patente per favore.
  favoreeska lah patenteh pehr favoreh
  Your license, please.

- Favorisca i documenti.
  favoreeska ee dokomentee
  Your papers.

AT THE GARAGE

Where is the nearest garage?	Dov'è la più vicina autofficina? *doveh lah pew veecheenah owtoffeecheenah*
Can you do repairs?	Effettuate le riparazioni? *effettwateh leh reeparatsyonee*
I need...	Ho bisogno di... *oh beezonyo dee*
...a new tire	...un nuovo pneumatico *oon nwovoh pneoomateekoh*
...a new exhaust	...un nuovo tubo di scarico *oon nwovoh tooboh dee skareekoh*
...a new windshield	...un nuovo parabrezza *oon nwovoh parabretsa*
...a new headlight	...una nuova lampadina *oonah nwovah lampadeenah*
...wiper blades	...spazzole del tergicristallo *spatsoleh del terjeekreestalloh*
Do you have one in stock?	Ne avete in magazzino? *neh aveteh een magadzeenoh*
Can you replace this?	Può sostituirlo/a? *pwo sosteetweerloh/ah*
The...is not working	Il/la...non funziona *eel/lah...non foontsyonah*
There is something wrong with the engine	Il motore non funziona bene *eel motoreh non foontsyonah beneh*
Is it serious?	È grave? *eh graveh*
When will it be ready?	Quando sarà pronta? *kwandoh sarah prontah*
How much will it cost?	Quanto costerà? *kwantoh kosterah*

CAR BREAKDOWN

My car has broken down	La mia automobile è in panne *lah meeah owtomobeeleh eh een panneh*
Please can you help me?	Mi può aiutare? *mee pwo ayewtareh*
Please come to...	Venga a... *vengah ah*
I have a flat tire	Ho una gomma a terra *oh oonah gommah ah terrah*
Can you help change the wheel?	Mi può aiutare a cambiare la ruota? *mee pwo ayewtareh ah kambyareh lah rwotah*
I need a new tire	Ho bisogno di un nuovo pneumatico *oh beezonyo dee oon nwovoh pneoomateekoh*
My car won't start	La mia auto non si accende *lah meeah owtoh non see atchendeh*
The engine is overheating	Il motore si sta surriscaldando *eel motoreh see stah sooreeskaldandoh*
Can you fix it?	Può aggiustarla? *pwo adjoostarlah*

You may hear...

- **Ha bisogno di aiuto?**
  ah beezonyo dee ayewtoh
  Do you need any help?

- **Qual è il problema?**
  kwaleh eel problemah
  What is the problem?

- **Ha la ruota di scorta?**
  ah lah rwotah dee skortah
  Do you have a spare tire?

LOST PROPERTY

I've lost…	Ho smarrito… *oh smareetoh*
…my money	…il mio denaro *eel meeoh denaroh*
…my keys	…le chiavi *leh kyavee*
…my glasses	…gli occhiali *lyee okyalee*
My luggage is missing	Il mio bagaglio è smarrito *eel meeoh bagalyo eh smareetoh*
My suitcase has been damaged	La mia valigia è stata danneggiata *la meeah valeeja eh statah dannedjatah*

il portafoglio
eel portafolyoh
wallet

il portamonete
eel portamoneteh
change purse

la valigetta
lah valeejettah
briefcase

la borsa
lah borsah
handbag

la valigia
lah valeejah
suitcase

il traveller's cheque
eel travellers cheque
traveler's check

la carta di credito
lah kartah dee kredeetoh
credit card

il passaporto
eel passaportoh
passport

la fotocamera
lah fotokamerah
camera

il cellulare
eel chelloolareh
cell phone

I need to call my insurance company	Devo telefonare alla mia agenzia assicurativa *devoh telefonareh allah meeah ajentsya asseekoorateevah*
Can I put a stop on my credit cards?	Posso bloccare le mie carte di credito? *possoh blokareh leh mee-eh karteh dee kredeetoh*
My name is…	Mi chiamo… *mee kyamoh*
My policy number is…	Il numero della polizza è… *eel noomeroh dellah poleedza eh*
My address is…	Il mio indirizzo è… *eel meeo eendeereedzo eh*
My contact number is…	Il mio numero di telefono è… *eel meeoh noomeroh dee telefono eh*
My email address is…	Il mio indirizzo e-mail è… *eel meeoh eendeereedzo emayl eh*

MENU GUIDE

This guide lists the most common terms you may encounter on Italian menus or when shopping for food. If you can't find an exact phrase, try looking up its component parts.

A

abbacchio alla romana Roman-style spring lamb
acciughe sott'olio anchovies in oil
aceto vinegar
acqua water
acqua minerale gassata sparkling mineral water
acqua minerale non gassata still mineral water
acqua naturale still mineral water, tap water
affettato misto variety of cold, sliced meats
affogato al caffè hot espresso on ice cream
aglio garlic
agnello lamb
albicocche apricots
al forno roast
amatriciana chopped bacon and tomato sauce
ananas pineapple
anatra duck
anatra all'arancia duck in orange sauce
anguilla in umido stewed eel
anguria watermelon
antipasti appetizers
antipasti misti mixed appetizers
aperitivo aperitif
aragosta lobster
arancia orange
aranciata orangeade; fresh orange juice
aringa herring
arrosto roast

arrosto di tacchino roast turkey
asparagi asparagus
avocado all'agro avocado with dressing

B

baccalà dried cod
baccalà alla vicentina Vicentine-style dried cod
bagnacauda vegetables (often raw) in a sauce of oil, garlic, and anchovy
Barbaresco dry red wine from Piedmont
Barbera dry red wine from Piedmont
Bardolino dry red wine from the Veneto region
Barolo dark, dry red wine from Piedmont
basilico basil
bavarese ice-cream cake; dessert made with cream
Bel Paese soft, white cheese
besciamella white sauce
bignè cream puff
birra beer
birra chiara light beer, lager
birra grande large beer
birra piccola small beer
birra scura dark beer
bistecca ai ferri grilled steak
bistecca (di manzo) steak
bolognese meat and tomato sauce
braciola di maiale pork steak
branzino al forno baked sea bass

brasato braised beef with herbs

bresaola dried, salted beef eaten with oil and lemon

brioche type of croissant

brodo clear broth

brodo vegetale clear vegetable broth

bucatini long tube pasta

budino pudding

burro butter

burro di acciughe anchovy butter

C

Caciotta tender, white cheese from Central Italy

caffè coffee

caffè corretto espresso with a dash of liqueur

caffè latte half coffee, half hot milk

caffè lungo weak espresso

caffè macchiato espresso with a dash of milk

caffè ristretto strong espresso

calamari in umido stewed squid

calamaro squid

calzone folded pizza with tomato and cheese

camomilla camomile tea

cannella cinnamon

cannelloni al forno baked pasta rolls filled with meat

cappuccino espresso with frothy milk sprinkled with cocoa powder

capretto al forno roast kid

carbonara sauce of egg, bacon, and cheese

carciofi artichokes

carciofini sott'olio baby artichokes in oil

carne meat

carote carrots

carpaccio finely sliced beef fillet with oil, lemon, and parmesan

carré di maiale al forno roast pork loin

cassata siciliana ice-cream cake with chocolate, glacé fruit, and ricotta

castagne chestnuts

cavoletti di Bruxelles Brussels sprouts

cavolfiore cauliflower

cavolo cabbage

cefalo gray mullet

cernia grouper (fish)

cetriolo cucumber

charlotte ice-cream cake with biscuits and fruit

Chianti dark red Tuscan wine

cicoria chicory

cicorino small chicory plants

ciliege cherries

cime di rapa sprouting broccoli

cioccolata chocolate

cioccolata calda hot chocolate

cipolle onions

cocktail di gamberetti shrimp cocktail

conchiglie alla marchigiana pasta shells in tomato sauce with ham, celery, carrot, and parsley

coniglio rabbit

coniglio in umido stewed rabbit

consommé clear broth

contorni vegetables

coperto cover charge

coppa cured neck of pork

costata alla fiorentina T-bone veal steak

costata di manzo T-bone beef steak

cotechino spiced pork sausage for boiling

cotoletta veal, pork, or lamb chop

cotoletta ai ferri grilled veal or pork chop

cotoletta alla milanese veal chop in breadcrumbs

cotoletta alla valdostana veal chop with ham and cheese, in breadcrumbs

cotolette di agnello lamb chops

cotolette di maiale pork chops

cozze mussels

cozze alla marinara mussels in white wine

crema custard dessert made with eggs and milk

crema al caffè coffee custard dessert

crema al cioccolato chocolate custard dessert

crema di funghi cream of mushroom soup

crema di piselli cream of pea soup

crema pasticciera confectioner's custard

crêpes Suzette pancakes flambéed with orange sauce

crescente fried bread made with flour, lard, and eggs

crespelle savory pancakes

crostata di frutta fruit tart

D, E

dadi bouillon cubes

datteri dates

degustazione di vini wine tasting

dentice al forno baked dentex (type of sea bream)

digestivo digestive liqueur

Dolcelatte creamy blue cheese

dolci sweets, desserts, cakes

endivia belga white chicory

entrecôte (di manzo) beef entrecote

espresso strong, black coffee

F

fagiano pheasant

fagioli beans

fagioli borlotti in umido borlotti borlotti beans in tomatoes and vegetables

fagiolini long, green beans

faraona guinea fowl

farcito stuffed

fegato liver

fegato alla veneta liver in butter with onions

fegato con salvia e burro liver in butter and sage

fettuccine ribbon-shaped pasta

fichi figs

filetti di pesce persico fillets of perch

filetti di sogliola fillets of sole

filetto ai ferri grilled fillet of beef

filetto al cognac fillet of beef flambé

filetto al pepe verde fillet of beef with green peppercorns

filetto al sangue rare fillet of beef

filetto ben cotto well-done fillet of beef

filetto (di manzo) fillet of beef

filetto medio medium-cooked fillet of beef

finocchi gratinati fennel au gratin

finocchio fennel

fonduta cheese fondue

formaggi misti variety of cheeses

fragole strawberries

fragole con gelato/panna strawberries and ice cream/cream

frappé fruit or milk shake with crushed ice

Frascati dry white wine from area around Rome

frittata type of omelette

frittata alle erbe herb omelette

fritto deep fried

fritto misto mixed seafood in batter

frittura di pesce variety of fried fish

frutta fruit

frutta alla fiamma fruit flambé

frutta secca dried nuts and raisins

frutti di bosco mixture of strawberries, raspberries, mulberries, etc

frutti di mare seafood

funghi mushrooms

funghi trifolati mushrooms fried in garlic and parsley

G

gamberetti shrimps

gamberi prawns

gamberoni king prawns

gazzosa clear lemonade

gelatina jelly

gelato ice cream

gelato di crema vanilla-flavored ice cream

gelato di frutta fruit-flavored ice cream

gnocchetti verdi agli spinaci e al gorgonzola small flour, potato, and spinach dumplings with melted gorgonzola

gnocchi small flour and potato dumplings

gnocchi alla romana small milk and semolina dumplings with butter

Gorgonzola strong blue cheese from Lombardy

grancevola spiny spider crab

granchio crab

granita sorbet made of sweetened syrup

grigliata di pesce grilled fish

grigliata mista mixed grill (meat or fish)

grissini thin, crisp breadsticks

Gruviera Gruyère cheese

I

indivia endive

insalata salad

insalata caprese salad of tomatoes and mozzarella

insalata di funghi porcini boletus mushroom salad

insalata di mare seafood salad

insalata di nervetti boiled beef or veal tendons served cold with beans and pickles

insalata di pomodori tomato salad

insalata di riso rice salad

insalata mista mixed salad

insalata russa Russian salad

insalata verde green salad

involtini meat rolls stuffed with ham and herbs

L

lamponi raspberries

lasagne al forno layers of pasta baked in meat sauce with cheese

latte milk

latte macchiato con cioccolato hot milk sprinkled with cocoa

lattuga lettuce

leggero light

legumi legumes

lemonsoda sparkling lemon drink

lenticchie lentils

lepre hare

limonata lemon-flavored fizzy drink

limone lemon

lingua tongue

M

macedonia di frutta fruit salad

maiale pork

maionese mayonnaise

mandarino mandarin

mandorla almond

manzo beef
marroni large chestnuts
Marsala fortified wine
marzapane marzipan
Mascarpone soft, mild
  cheese
medaglioni di vitello
  veal medallions
mela apple
melagrana pomegranate
melanzane eggplant
melone melon
menta mint
meringata meringue pie
merluzzo cod
merluzzo alla pizzaiola
  cod in tomato sauce with
  anchovies and capers
merluzzo in bianco cod
  with oil and lemon
messicani in gelatina rolls
  of veal in jelly
millefoglie pastry layered
  with custard
minestra in brodo
  noodle soup
minestrone vegetable soup
  with rice or pasta
mirtilli bilberries
more mulberries or
  blackberries
moscato sweet wine
mousse al cioccolato
  chocolate mousse
Mozzarella soft cheese
mozzarella in carrozza
  fried slices of bread and
  mozzarella

N, O

nasello hake
nocciole hazelnuts
noce moscata nutmeg
noci walnuts
nodino veal chop
olio oil
origano oregano
ossobuco stewed shin
  of veal
ostriche oysters

P

paglia e fieno mixed plain
  and green tagliatelle
paillard di manzo slices
  of grilled beef
paillard di vitello slices
  of grilled veal
pane bread
panino filled roll; bread roll
panna cream
parmigiana di melanzane
  aubergines baked with
  cheese
pasta al forno pasta baked
  in white sauce and grated
  cheese
pasta e fagioli thick soup
  with borlotti beans and
  pasta rings
pasta e piselli pasta
  with peas
pasticcio di fegato d'oca
  baked pasta dish with
  goose liver
pasticcio di lepre baked
  pasta dish with hare
pasticcio di maccheroni
  baked macaroni
pastina in brodo soup with
  small pasta
patate potatoes
patate al forno/arrosto
  roast potatoes
patate fritte french fries
patate in insalata potato
  salad
Pecorino strong, hard
  cheese made from sheep's
  milk
penne pasta quills
penne ai quattro formaggi
  pasta with four cheeses
  sauce
penne all'arrabbiata pasta
  with tomato and chilli
  pepper sauce
penne panna e prosciutto
  pasta with cream and ham
  sauce
pepe pepper (spice)

peperoncino crushed chilli pepper

peperoni peppers

peperoni ripieni stuffed peppers

peperoni sott'olio peppers in oil

pera pear

pesca peach

pesce fish

pesce al cartoccio fish baked in foil with herbs

pesce in carpione marinaded fish

pesto sauce of basil, pine nuts, Parmesan, garlic, and oil

Pinot dry white wine from the Veneto region

pinzimonio sauce with oil and vinegar served with raw vegetables

piselli peas

piselli al prosciutto peas with ham and basil

pizzaiola slices of cooked beef in tomato sauce, oregano, and anchovies

pizzoccheri alla Valtellinese pasta strips with vegetables and cheese

polenta boiled cornmeal left to set and sliced

polenta e osei polenta with small birds

polenta pasticciata layers of polenta, tomato sauce, and cheese

pollo chicken

pollo alla cacciatora chicken in white wine with onions and carrots

pollo alla diavola deep-fried chicken pieces

polpette meatballs

polpettone meatloaf

pomodori tomatoes

pomodori ripieni stuffed tomatoes

pompelmo grapefruit

porri leeks

prezzemolo parsley

primi piatti first courses

prosciutto cotto cooked ham

prosciutto crudo type of cured ham

prugne plums

punte di asparagi all'agro asparagus tips in oil and lemon

purè di patate mashed potatoes

puttanesca tomato sauce with anchovies, capers, and black olives

Q, R

quaglie quails

radicchio red chicory

ragù meat-based sauce

rapanelli radishes

ravioli stuffed pasta parcels

ravioli al pomodoro meat ravioli in tomato sauce

razza skate

Ricotta type of cottage cheese

risi e bisi risotto with peas and ham

riso rice

risotto rice cooked in stock

risotto alla castellana risotto with mushroom, ham, cream, and cheese

risotto alla milanese risotto with saffron

risotto al nero di seppia risotto with cuttlefish ink

risotto al tartufo truffle risotto

roast-beef all'inglese thinly sliced cold roast beef

Robiola type of soft cheese from Lombardy

rognone trifolato kidney in garlic, oil, and parsley

rosatello/rosato rosé wine

rosmarino rosemary

S

salame salami

sale salt

salmone affumicato smoked salmon

salsa cocktail/rosa mayonnaise and ketchup sauce for fish and seafood

salsa di pomodoro tomato sauce

salsa tartara tartar sauce

salsa vellutata white sauce made with clear broth

salsa verde sauce for meat, with parsley and oil

salsiccia sausage

salsiccia di cinghiale wild boar sausage

salsiccia di maiale pork sausage

saltimbocca alla romana slices of veal stuffed with ham and sage and fried

salvia sage

sambuca (con la mosca) aniseed-flavor liqueur served with a coffee bean

sarde ai ferri grilled sardines

scaloppine veal cutlets

scaloppine al prezzemolo veal cutlets with parsley

scamorza alla griglia grilled soft cheese

scampi alla griglia grilled scampi

secco dry

secondi piatti second courses, main courses

sedano celery

selvaggina game

semifreddo cake or dessert often containing cream and served chilled

senape mustard

seppie in umido stewed cuttlefish

servizio compreso service charge included

servizio escluso service charge excluded

Soave dry white wine from the Veneto region

sogliola sole

sogliola ai ferri grilled sole

sogliola al burro sole cooked in butter

sogliola alla mugnaia sole cooked in flour and butter

sorbetto sorbet, soft ice cream

soufflé al formaggio cheese soufflé

soufflé al prosciutto ham soufflé

speck cured, smoked ham

spezzatino di vitello veal stew

spiedini assorted chunks of spit-cooked meat or fish

spinaci spinach

spinaci all'agro spinach with oil and lemon

spremuta di… freshly squeezed…juice

spumante sparkling wine

Stracchino soft cheese from Lombardy

stracciatella soup of beaten eggs in clear broth

strudel di mele apple strudel

stufato braised

succo di… …juice

sugo al tonno tomato sauce with tuna, garlic, and parsley

T

tacchino ripieno stuffed turkey

tagliata finely cut beef fillet cooked in the oven

tagliatelle thin ribbon-shaped pasta

tagliatelle rosse tagliatelle made with beets

tagliatelle verdi tagliatelle made with spinach

tagliolini thin soup noodles

tartine small sandwiches

tartufo ice cream covered in cocoa or chocolate; truffle

tè tea

tiramisù dessert with coffee-soaked sponge, Marsala, Mascarpone, and cocoa powder

tonno tuna

torta tart, flan

torta di ricotta type of cheesecake

torta salata savory flan

tortellini pasta shapes filled with minced pork, ham, Parmesan, and nutmeg

trancio di palombo smooth dogfish steak

trancio di pesce spada swordfish steak

trenette col pesto flat spaghetti with pesto sauce

triglia mullet (fish)

trippa tripe

trota trout

trota affumicata smoked trout

trota al burro trout cooked in butter

trota alle mandorle trout with almonds

trota bollita boiled trout

U

uccelletti small birds wrapped in bacon, served on cocktail sticks

uova eggs

uova alla coque soft-boiled eggs

uova al tegamino con pancetta fried eggs and bacon

uova farcite eggs with tuna, capers, and mayonnaise filling

uova sode hard-boiled eggs

uva grapes

uva bianca white grapes

uva nera black grapes

V

vellutata di asparagi creamed asparagus with egg yolks

vellutata di piselli creamed peas with egg yolks

verdura vegetables

vermicelli long, very fine, thin pasta

vino wine

vino bianco white wine

vino da dessert dessert wine

vino da pasto table wine

vino da tavola table wine

vino rosso red wine

vitello veal

vitello tonnato cold sliced veal in tuna, anchovy, oil, and lemon sauce

vongole clams

W, Z

würstel hot dog

zabaglione creamy dessert of eggs, sugar, and Marsala

zafferano saffron

zucca pumpkin

zucchero sugar

zucchine zucchini

zucchine al pomodoro zucchini in tomato, garlic and parsley sauce

zucchine ripiene stuffed zucchini

zuccotto ice-cream cake with sponge fingers, cream, and chocolate

zuppa soup

zuppa di cipolle onion soup

zuppa di cozze mussel soup

zuppa di lenticchie lentil soup

zuppa di pesce fish soup

zuppa di verdura vegetable soup

zuppa inglese trifle

DICTIONARY ENGLISH–ITALIAN

The gender of an Italian noun is shown by the word for "the": **il** or **lo** (masculine), **la** (feminine), and their plural forms **i** or **gli** (masculine) and **le** (feminine). When **lo** or **la** are abbreviated to **l'** in front of a vowel or **h**, the gender of the noun is shown by the abbreviation **(m)** or **(f)** after it.

A

about **circa**
accident **l'incidente (m)**
account number **il numero di conto**
adapter **l'adattatore (m)**
address **l'indirizzo (m)**
adhesive bandage **il cerotto**
adult **l'adulto (m)**
aerobics **l'aerobica (f)**
after **dopo**
afternoon **il pomeriggio**
again **ancora**
air conditioning **l'aria condizionata (f)**
airplane **l'aeroplano (m)**
airmail **la posta aerea**
airport **l'aeroporto (m)**
aisle seat **il posto vicino al corridoio**
all **tutto**
allergic **allergico/a**
almost **quasi**
alone **solo/a**
already **già**
ambulance **l'ambulanza (f)**
American **americano/a (m/f)**
and **e**
ankle **la caviglia**
another **altro/a**
answering machine **la segreteria telefonica**
antibiotics **gli antibiotici**
anything **qualcosa**
anything **niente**
appointment **l'appuntamento (m)**
April **aprile**
apron **il grembiule**
arm **il braccio**

armband **il bracciolo**
arrive (verb) **arrivare**
arrivals hall **gli arrivi**
art gallery **la galleria d'arte**
arthritis **l'artrite (f)**
artificial sweetener **il dolcificante**
as **come**
asthma **l'asma (f)**
at **a**
audio guide **la guida audio**
August **agosto**
Australia **Australia (f)**
automatic ticket machine **la biglietteria automatica**
awful **orribile**

B

babysitting **il servizio di babysitting**
back (body) **la schiena**
back (not front of) **la parte posteriore**
backpack **lo zaino**
bad **cattivo/a**
bag **la borsa**
baggage allowance **il bagaglio consentito**
baggage claim **il ritiro bagagli**
baggage claim check **la ricevuta dei bagagli**
bakery **la panetteria**
balcony **il balcone**
ball **la palla**
ballet **la danza**
bandage **la benda**
bank **la banca**
bank account **il conto bancario**

bank manager il direttore della banca
bar il bar
baseball glove il guanto da baseball
basket il cestino
basketball la palla da baske
bathtub il bagno
bath robe l'accappatoio (m)
bathroom il bagno
battery la batteria
be (verb) essere
beach la spiaggia
beach ball il pallone da spiaggia
beach towel il telo da spiaggia
beautiful bello/a
bed il letto
bee l'ape (f)
before prima di
beginner principiante (m/f)
behind dietro a
below sotto
belt la cintura
beneath sotto
beside vicino a
bicycle la bicicletta
big grande
bikini il bikini
bill; check il conto
black nero/a
blanket la coperta
blender il frullatore
blood pressure la pressione sanguigna
blood test le analisi del sangue
blue blu
board (verb) imbarcarsi
boarding gate l'uscita d'imbarco (f)
boarding pass la carta d'imbarco
boat la barca
body il corpo
body lotion la crema per il corpo
book il libro
book store la libreria

book (verb) prenotare
boot (car) il bagagliaio
boot lo stivale
bottle la bottiglia
bottle opener l'apribottiglie (m)
boutique la boutique
bowl la scodella
box la scatola
boy il ragazzo
boyfriend il fidanzato
bracelet il bracciale
breakdown il guasto
breakfast la colazione
briefcase la valigetta
British britannico/a
broken rotto/a
bruise l'ematoma (m)
brush (cleaning) la scopa
bubblebath il bagnoschiuma
bucket lo secchi
bumper il paraurti
burgle (verb) svaligiare
burn la bruciatura
bus l'autobus (m)
bus station la stazione degli autobus
bus stop la fermata dell'autobus
business, on per lavoro
bust il busto
butcher's la macelleria
buy (verb) comprare
by da; vicino a

C

cabin la cabina
cable car la funivia
café il bar
calm calmo/a
camera la fotocamera
camera bag la borsa per fotocamera
camper van il camper
camping kettle il bollitore da campeggio
camping stove il fornetto da campeggio
campsite il campeggio
can (verb) potere

can (noun) la scatoletta

can opener l'apribottiglie (m)

Canada il Canada

canoe la canoa

capsule la capsula

car la macchina

car rental desk l'ufficio dell'autonoleggio (m)

carry (verb) portare

carry out da portar via

cart il carrello

cash il denaro

cash (verb) riscuotere

cash machine il sportello bancomat

casino il casinò

casserole dish la casseruola

castle il castello

catamaran il catamarano

cathedral la cattedrale

CD il CD

cell phone il cellulare

central heating il riscaldamento centralizzato

center il centro

chair lift la seggiovia

change (verb) cambiare

change purse il portamonete

changing room lo spogliatoio

channel (TV) il canale

charge (verb) addebitare

check l'assegno (m)

checkbook il libretto degli assegni

check card la carta assegni

check in il check-in

check out (hotel) lasciare

check-out (supermarket) la cassa

cheek la guancia

cheers! cin cin!

chest il torace

chewing gum la gomma da masticare

child bambino/a (m/f)

chin il mento

church la chiesa

cigarette la sigaretta

city la città

clean pulito/a

close (near) vicino

close (verb) chiudere

closed chiuso/a

clothes gli abiti

cloudy nuvoloso/a

clubbing andare in discoteca

coast la costa

coat il cappotto

coat hanger l'appendiabiti (m)

colander il colino

cold (illness) il raffreddore

cold freddo/a

collect call la chiamata a carico del destinatario

coloring pencil la matita colorata

come (verb) venire

comic il fumetto

compartment il scompartimento

compass la bussola

complain (verb) reclamare

computer il computer

concert il concerto

concourse l'atrio (m)

conditioner il balsamo

constipation la stitichezza

consul il console

consulate il consolato

contact number il numero di telefono

contents il contenuto

cookie sheet la teglia da forno

cooler il frigo portatile

corkscrew il cavatappi

cough la tosse

country il paese

courier il corriere

course il piatto

cream (lotion) la crema

credit card la carta di credito

crib il lettino

crime il reato

cross trainer l'ellittica (f)

cufflinks **gli gemelli**
cup **la tazza**
cut **il taglio**
cutlery **le posate**
cycling helmet **il casco**

D

damaged **danneggiato/a**
dancing **ballare**
dashboard **il cruscotto**
daughter **la figlia**
day **il giorno**
December **dicembre**
deck chair **la sedia a sdraio**
degrees **gradi**
delayed **ritardo**
delicatessen **la gastronomia**
delicious **delizioso/a**
dentist **la dentista**
deodorant **il deodorante**
departure board **il tabellone delle partenze**
departures hall **le partenze**
deposit **il deposito**
desk **la scrivania**
detergent **il detergente**
develop (film) **sviluppare**
diabetic **diabetico/a**
diarrhea **la diarrea**
diesel **il diesel**
digital camera **la fotocamera digitale**
dining car **la carrozza ristorante**
dinner **la cena**
disabled parking **il parcheggio per disabili**
dish **il piatto**
divorced **divorziato/a**
do (verb) **fare**
doctor **il dottore**
doctor's office **l'ambulatorio (m)**
dog **il cane**
doll **la bambola**
door **la porta**
double bed **il letto matrimoniale**
double room **la camera doppia**

drawing **il disegno**
dress **l'abito (m)**
dressing **la fasciatura**
drink (verb) **bere**
drink (noun) **la bibita**
drive (verb) **guidare**
driver's license **la patente di guida**
dry (wine) **secco**
dry (day; clothes) **asciutto**
during **durante**
dust pan **la paletta**
duty-free shop **il negozio duty-free**
DVD player **il lettore DVD**

E

each (every) **ogni**
each **ciascuno**
early **presto**
ear **l'orecchio (m)**
east **l'est (m)**
eat (verb) **mangiare**
eight **otto**
elbow **il gomito**
electric razor **il rasoio elettrico**
electrician **l'elettricista (m)**
electricity **l'elettricità (f)**
elevator **l'ascensore (m)**
eleven **undici**
email **l'e-mail (f)**
email address **l'indirizzo e-mail (m)**
embassy **l'ambasciata (f)**
emergency room **il Pronto Soccorso**
emergency services **gli servizi di emergenza**
empty **vuoto/a**
engine **il motore**
English **inglese**
engraving **l'incisione (f)**
enjoy (verb) **divertirsi**
entrance **l'entrata (f)**
entrance/exit ramp **la bretella**
entrance ticket **il biglietto d'entrata**
envelope **la busta**
epileptic **epilettico/a**

equipment l'attrezzatura (f)
euro l'euro (m)
evening la sera
evening dress l'abito
   da sera (m)
examine (verb) esaminare
exchange rate il tasso
   di cambio
excursion l'escursione (f)
exercise bike la bicicletta
exhaust (car) la marmitta
exit l'uscita (f)
expensive caro/a
express service il servizio
   espresso
extension cord la prolunga
extra extra
eye l'occhio (m)

F

face il viso
fairground il luna park
fall l'autunno (m)
family la famiglia
family room la camera
   familiare
family ticket il biglietto
   famiglia
fan il ventilatore
far lontano
fare la tariffa
fast veloce
father il padre
favorite preferito/a
February febbraio
ferry il traghetto
fifty cinquanta
film (camera) il rullino
find (verb) trovare
fine (legal) la multa
finger il dito
finish (verb) finire
fire alarm l'allarme
   antincendio (m)
fire engine l'autopompa (f)
fire extinguisher l'estintore
   (m)
firefighter il pompiere
first primo/a
fish il pesce

fish seller il pescivendolo
five cinque
fix (verb) riparare
flash gun il flash
flashlight la torcia
flash photography
   la fotografia con il flash
flat tire la gomma a terra
flight il volo
flight attendant l'assistente
   di volo (f)
flip-flop l'infradito (f)
flippers le pinne
float la tavoletta
flu l'influenza (f)
food il cibo
foot il piede
for per
fork la forchetta
forty quaranta
four quattro
fracture la frattura
free (not occupied) libero/a
free (no charge) gratis
fresh fresco/a
Friday venerdì
fridge-freezer il frigorifero
   congelatore
friend l'amico/a (m/f)
from da
front; in front of davanti;
   di fronte a
frying pan la padella
fuel gauge l'indicatore di
   livello del carburante (m)
full pieno/a
furniture store il negozio
   di arredamento
fuse box la scatola
   dei fusibili

G

gallery (theater) la galleria
game il gioco
garage il garage
garbage can la pattumiera
garden il giardino
garlic l'aglio (m)
gas il gas
gasoline il carburante

gas station la stazione di servizio
gate il cancello
gear shift la leva del cambio
get off (verb) scendere
gift il regalo
gift shop il negozio di articoli da regalo
girl la ragazza
girlfriend la fidanzata
give (verb) dare
glass il vetro
glass (drinking) il bicchiere
glasses gli occhiali
gloss lucido
go (verb) andare
go out (verb) uscire
goggles gli occhialini
golf il golf
golf ball la palla da golf
golf club la mazza
golf course il campo da golf
golf tee il tee
good buono/a
goodbye arrivederci
good evening buonasera
good night buonanotte
grater la grattugia
graze l'escoriazione (f)
Great Britain la Gran Bretagna
green verde
greengrocery il fruttivendolo
grill pan la griglia
group il gruppo
guarantee la garanzia
guest l'ospite (m/f)
guide (person) la guida
guidebook la guida
guided tour la visita guidata
gym la palestra

H

hair i capelli
hairdryer l'asciugacapelli (m)
half la metà; mezzo/a (adj)
hand la mano
hand luggage il bagaglio a mano

handbag la borsa
handle la maniglia
happen (verb) succedere
happy contento/a; felice
harbor il porto
hardware store la ferramenta
hatchback il portellone
hate (verb) odiare
have (verb) avere
hayfever il raffreddore da fieno
hazard lights le frecce lampeggianti
he egli; lui
head la testa
headache il mal di testa
head rest il poggiatesta
headlight i fari
health la salute
health insurance l'assicurazione sanitaria
hear (verb) sentire
heart condition la patologia cardiaca
heater l'impianto di riscaldamento (m)
heating il riscaldamento
heel il tallone
hello ciao; buongiorno
hello (on phone) pronto
help (verb) aiutare
her (object) lei
her (possessive) suo/sua (sing)/sue/suoi (plural)
here qui
high blood pressure la pressione arteriosa elevata
high chair il seggiolone
high-speed train il treno ad alta velocità
highway l'autostrada (f)
hiking l'escursionismo (m)
hiking boots gli scarponi
him lui
hire (verb) noleggiare
hold (verb) tenere
holdall la sacca da viaggio
hood (car) il cofano

horn il clacson
horseback riding andare a
  cavallo
hospital l'ospedale (m)
hot caldo/a
hotel l'albergo (m)
hour l'ora (f)
house la casa
hovercraft il hovercraft
how much? quanto?
how come?
how many? quanti/e?
humid umido/a
hundred cento
hurry (verb) affrettarsi
husband il marito
hydrofoil l'aliscafo (m)
hydrant l'idrante (m)

I

I (1st person) io
ice il ghiaccio
icy ghiacciato/a
ID la carta d'identità
illness la malattia
in in
in-flight meal il pasto a bordo
inhaler l'inalatore (m)
injection l'iniezione (f)
injure (verb) ferirsi
insect repellent il repellente
  per gli insetti
insurance l'assicurazione (f)
insurance company l'agenzia
  assicurativa (f)
insurance policy la polizza
  assicurativa
intensive care unit il reparto
  di terapia intensiva
interest (verb) interessare
interesting interessante
internet l'Internet (m)
internet café l'Internet cafè
interpreter l'interprete (m/f)
inventory l'inventario (m)
iPod l'iPod (m)
iron il ferro da stiro
ironing board l'asse
  a stiro (f)
it esso/a; lo/la/l'; gli/le

Italian italiano/a
Italy l'Italia (f)

J

jacket la giacca
January gennaio
jaw la mascella
jazz club il jazz club
jeans i jeans
jellyfish la medusa
jet ski il moto d'acqua
jewelry store il gioielliere
jewelry la gioielleria
July luglio
June giugno

K

keep straight andare dritto
kettle il bollitore
key la chiave
keyboard la tastiera
kilo il chilo
kilometer il chilometro
kitchen la cucina
knee il ginocchio
knife il coltello
knock down (verb) colpire
know (people) conoscere
know (a fact) sapere

L

lake il lago
laptop il computer portatile
large grande
last ultimo/a
late tardi; in ritardo
lawyer l'avvocato (m)
leak la perdita
leave (verb) lasciare; partire
left sinistra
left luggage il deposito
  bagagli
leisure activities le attività
  del tempo libero
leg la gamba
lens la lente
license plate il numero
  di targa
lifebuoy il salvagente
lifeguard il bagnino

life jacket il giubbotto di salvataggio
lift pass il pass per lo ski-lift
light leggero/a
light (noun) la luce
light (verb) accendere
light bulb la lampadina
lighter l'accendino (m)
lighthouse il faro
like (verb) piacere
line la linea
list la lista
listen (verb) ascoltare
little poco; piccolo
local locale
lock il lucchetto
lock (verb) chiudere a chiave
log on (verb) connettersi
log out (verb) disconnettersi
long lungo
look (verb) guardare
lose (verb) perdere
lost property l'ufficio oggetti smarriti (m)
loung chair il lettino sdraio
love (verb) amare
luggage il bagaglio
lunch il pranzo

M

magazine la rivista
mail la posta
mail (verb) spedire la posta
mailbox la cassetta delle lettere
make (verb) fare
mallet il maglio
man l'uomo (m)
manual il manuale
manuscript il manoscritto
many molti/e
map la mappa; la cartina
marina il porticciolo
market il mercato
married sposato/a
match (sport) la partita
match (light) il fiammifero
matte opaco/a
mattress il materasso

May maggio
mechanic il meccanico
medicine la medicina
medium mezzo
memory card la scheda di memoria
memory stick la chiavetta USB
mend (verb) riparare
menu il menù
message il messaggio
microwave il forno a microonde
middle mezzo
midnight mezzanotte
mini bar il mini bar
minute il minuto
mistake l'errore (m)
misty nebbioso/a
mixed misto/a
mixing bowl l'insalatiera (f)
mole (medical) il neo
Monday lunedì
money il denaro; i soldi
month il mese
monument il monumento
mooring l'ormeggio (m)
more più
morning il mattino
mother la madre
motorcycle la motocicletta
mountain la montagna
mountain bike la mountain bike
mouse (computer) il mouse
mouth la bocca
mouthwash il collutorio
movie theater il cinema
much molto
museum il museo
music la musica
musician il musicista
must (verb) dovere
my mio/mia/mie/miei
myself mi; me stesso/a

N

nail l'unghia (f)
nail clippers i tagliaunghie
nail scissors le forbicine per

le unghie
name il mome
napkin il tovagliolo
nausea la nausea
neck il collo
necklace la collana
need (verb) aver bisogno
news kiosk l'edicola (f)
newspaper il giornale
never mai
next prossimo/a
next to vicino a
new nuovo/a
nice bello/a; piacevole
night la notte
nightclub il nightclub
nine nove
no no
noon mezzogiorno
north il nord
nose nil naso
nosebleed il sangue
  dal naso
not non
November novembre
number il numero
nurse l'infermiera (f)
nursery slopes le discese
  per i principianti

O

October ottobre
of di
off spento/a
often spesso
oil l'olio (m)
ointment la pomata
on (light) acceso/a
on su
one uno/a
online online
only solamente
open aperto/a
open (verb) aprire
opening hours l'orario
  di apertura (m)
opera l'opera (f)
opera house il teatro
  dell'opera
operation l'intervento

chirurgico (m)
opposite davanti; di fronte
or o
orange (color) arancione
order l'ordine (m)
order (verb) ordinare
other altro/a
our nostro/nostri/nostra/
  nostre
outside fuori
oven il forno
oven mitts i guanti
  da forno
over su; sopra
overnight tutta la notte
owe (verb) essere in debito

P

pack (verb) fare le valigie
pack il pacchetto
pain il dolore
painkiller l'antidolorifico (m)
painting il dipinto
pair la coppia
paper la carta
papers (ID) i documenti
park il parco
park (verb) parcheggiare
parking il parcheggio
parking lot il parcheggio
parking meter il parchimetro
passenger il passeggero
passport il passaporto
passport control il controllo
  passaporti
pay (verb) pagare
pay in (verb) effettuare
  un deposito
pedestrian crossing
  l'attraversamento
  pedonale (m)
peeler lo sbucciatore
pen la penna
pencil la matita
people la gente; le persone
perhaps forse
personal CD player il lettore
  CD
pet l'animale domestico
  (m)

pharmacist il farmacista

pharmacy la farmacia

phone il telefono

phone call la telefonata

phone card la carta telefonica

photo album l'album delle fotografie (m)

photograph la fotografia

photography la fotografia

pianist il pianista

picnic il picnic

picnic basket il cestino da picnic

picture frame la cornice

piece il pezzo

pilates pilates

pill la compressa

pillow il cuscino

pilot il pilota

PIN number il PIN

pink rosa

place il luogo

plate il piatto

platform il binario

play (games) (verb) giocare

playground l'area giochi (f)

please per favore

plug la spina

poles (ski) le racchette da sci

police la polizia

police car la volante

police station il commissariato

policeman il poliziotto

policewoman la poliziotta

policy la polizza

pool la piscina

porter il facchino

possible possibile

post office l'ufficio postale (m)

postcard la cartolina

postman il postino

prefer (verb) preferire

pregnant incinta

prescription la ricetta medica

present il regalo

price il prezzo

print (verb) stampare

print (photo) la stampa

program il programma

public holiday il giorno festivo

pump (bicycle) la pompa

put (verb) mettere

Q, R

quarter il quarto

quick rapido/a; veloce

quite abbastanza

radiator il radiatore

radio la radio

railroad la ferrovia

raining piovendo

rape la violenza carnale

rash l'eruzione (f)

razor il rasoio

read (verb) leggere

ready pronto/a

really veramente

receipt la ricevuta

recommend (verb) consigliare

record store il negozio di dischi

red rosso/a

reduction la riduzione

remote control il telecomando

rent (verb) affittare; noleggiare

repair (verb) riparare

report (noun) la denuncia

report (verb) denunciare

reservation la prenotazione

reserve (verb) prenotare; riservare

restaurant il ristorante

restroom il bagno

resuscitation la rianimazione

retired in pensione

return ticket il biglietto di andata e ritorno

rides le giostre

right (direction) destra

river il fiume

road la strada

road signs **segnali stradali (m pl)**
rob (verb) **derubare**
robbery **il furto**
roll (film) **il rullino**
roofrack **il bagagliaio**
room **la stanza; la camera**
room with twin beds **la camera a due letti**
round **rotondo/a**
rowing machine **il vogatore**

S

safari park **il parco safari**
safe **sicuro/a**
sailing **la vela**
sailboat **la barca a vela**
same **stesso/a**
sand **la sabbia**
sandals **i sandali**
satellite TV **la TV satellitare**
Saturday **sabato**
saucepan **la pentola**
saucer **il piattino**
say (verb) **dire**
scan **l'ecografia (f)**
scissors **le forbici**
sea **il mare**
season **la stagione**
seat **il posto; la sedia**
second **secondo/a**
sedan **la berlina**
see (verb) **vedere**
sell (verb) **vendere**
sell-by date **la data di scadenza**
send (verb) **inviare; mandare; spedire**
senior citizen **anziano/a**
separately **separatamente**
September **settembre**
serious **grave; serio/a**
serve (verb) **servire**
seven **sette**
shampoo **lo shampoo**
shaving foam **la schiuma da barba**
she **ella; lei**
shirt **la camicia**
shoe **la scarpa**

shopping **fare la spesa**
shopping mall **il centro commerciale**
shorts **i calzoncini**
shoulder **la spalla**
shower **la doccia**
shower gel **il docciaschiuma**
sick **malato/a**
side effect **l'effetto indesiderato (m)**
side plate **il piattino**
signpost **il cartello**
singer **cantante (m/f)**
single room **la camera singola**
single ticket **il biglietto di sola andata**
six **sei**
size **la taglia**
ski boots **gli scarponi da sci**
skiing **lo sci**
skin **la pelle**
skis **gli sci**
skirt **la gonna**
sleeper berth **la cuccetta**
sleeping bag **lo sacco a pelo**
slice **la fetta**
slickers **gli indumenti impermeabili**
slow **lento/a**
small **piccolo/a**
smoke (verb) **fumare**
smoke alarm **il rivelatore di fumo**
snack **lo spuntino**
snake **il serpente**
sneakers **le scarpe da ginnastica**
sneeze (verb) **starnutire**
snorkel **il boccaglio**
snow (verb) **nevicare**
snowboard **lo snowboard**
so **così**
soap **il sapone**
soccer (ball) **il pallone**
soccer (game) **il calcio**
socks **i calzini**
some **alcuni/e**
somebody **qualcuno/a**
something **qualcosa**

sometimes **qualche volta**
soon **presto**
sore **infiammato/a**
sorry **scusi**
south **il sud**
souvenir **il souvenir**
spare tyre **la ruota di scorta**
spatula **la spatola**
speak (verb) **parlare**
specialty **la specialità**
speed limit **il limite di velocità**
speedometer **il tachimetro**
splint **la stecca**
splinter **la scheggia**
spoon **il cucchiaio**
sport **lo sport**
sports center **il centro sportivo**
sprain **la distorsione**
spray **lo spray**
spring **la primavera**
square (in town) **la piazza**
squash (game) **lo squash**
stairs **le scale**
stamp **il francobollo**
start (verb) **cominciare**
station **la stazione**
statue **la statua**
stay **il soggiorno**
step machine **la step machine**
adhesive tape **lo scotch**
stolen **rubato/a**
stomach **lo stomaco**
stomach ache **il mal di stomaco**
stop (bus) **la fermata**
stop (verb) **fermare**
store **il negozio**
stormy **tempestoso/a**
street **la strada; la via**
street map **la cartina; la mappa**
string **la corda**
strong **forte**
student **studente/ studentessa (m/f)**
student card **la carta studenti**

stuffed animal **il peluche**
subway **la metropolitana**
suit **il completo**
suitcase **la valigia**
summer **l'estate (f)**
Sun **il sole**
sunburn **la bruciatura**
sunglasses **gli occhiali da sole**
sunhat **il cappello da sole**
suntan lotion **la lozione solare**
Sunday **domenica**
sunny **assolato/a**
sunscreen **il filtro solare**
supermarket **il supermercato**
suppositories **le supposte**
surf (verb) **fare surf**
surfboard **la tavola da surf**
sweater **il maglione**
swimming **il nuoto**
swimming pool **la piscina**
swimsuit **il costume**

T

table **il tavolo**
tablet **la compressa**
tailor **il sarto**
take (verb) **prendere**
taxi **il taxi**
taxi stand **il posteggio dei taxi**
teaspoon **il cucchiaino**
teeth **i denti**
telephone **il telefono**
telephone (verb) **telefonare**
telephone booth **la cabina del telefono**
television (set) **il televisore**
tell (verb) **dire**
temperature **la temperatura**
ten **dieci**
tennis **il tennis**
tennis ball **la palla da tennis**
tennis court **il campo da tennis**
tennis racket **la racchetta da tennis**

tent la tenda
tent peg il picchetto
terminal il terminal
than di
less meno
thank you grazie
that quello/a
the il/lo/la/i/gli/le
theater il teatro
their loro
then poi; allora
there is/are c'è/ci sono
thermostat termostato (m)
thief ladro (m)
think (verb) pensare
this questo/a
thirty trenta
thousand mille
three tre
throat la gola
through attraverso
thumb il pollice
Thursday giovedì
ticket il biglietto
tight stretto
time il tempo
timetable l'orario (m)
tire il pneumatico
tire pressure la pressione
  degli pneumatici
tobacco il tabacco
tobacco shop
  il tabaccaio (m)
today oggi
toe il dito del piede
toll il pedaggio
tomorrow domani
tonight stasera
too (excessively) troppo
toothache il mal di denti
toothbrush lo spazzolino
  da denti
toothpaste il dentifricio
tour il giro
tour guide la guida turistica
tourist turista (m/f)
tourist information office
  l'ufficio del turismo (m)
tow (verb) rimorchiare
towel l'asciugamano (m)

town la città
town center il centro
  della città
town hall il municipio
toy il giocattolo
traffic circle la rotatoria
traffic jam l'ingorgo
traffic lights il semaforo
train il treno
traveler's check il travellers
  cheque
trip la gita
try (verb) provare
t-shirt la T-shirt
Tuesday martedì
turn (verb) girare; voltare
turn off (verb) spegnere
twenty venti
two due

U

umbrella l'ombrello (m)
understand (verb) capire:
  comprendere
United States gli Stati Uniti
unleaded senza piombo
until fino a
up su
urgent urgente
us noi
use (verb) usare
useful utile
usual solito/a
usually generalmente

V

vacancy (room) la stanza
  libera
vacation la vacanza
vacuum flask il thermos
validate (verb) vidimare
valuables gli oggetti
  di valore
vegetarian vegetariano/a
Venetian blind la tenda
  veneziana
very molto
video game il videogioco
view la vista
village il villaggio

vineyard il vigneto
visa il visto
visiting hours l'orario delle visite
visitor il visitatore

W

wait (verb) aspettare
waiting room la sala d'attesa
waiter il cameriere
waitress la cameriera
wake-up call la sveglia telefonica
walk la passeggiata
wallet il portafoglio
want (verb) volere
ward la corsia
warm caldo/a
washing machine la lavatrice
wasp la vespa
watch (verb) guardare
water l'acqua (f)
waterfall la cascata
water-skiing lo sci d'acqua
water valve il rubinetto di arresto
we noi
weather il tempo
website il sito Web
Wednesday mercoledì
week la settimana
weekend il fine settimana
welcome benvenuto
well bene
west l'ovest (m)
wet bagnato/a
what? cosa?
wheel la ruota
wheelchair la sedia a rotelle
wheelchair access l'accesso per i disabili (m)
wheelchair ramp la rampa per i disabili
when? quando?
where? dove?
which? quale?
whisk rusta (f)
white bianco/a
who? chi?
why? perché?

widescreen TV il televisore a schermo panoramico
wife la moglie
wind il vento
window la finestra
window seat il posto vicino al finestrino
windshield la parabrezza
windshield wiper ' il tergicristallo
windsurfer surfista (m/f)
windy ventoso/a
wine il vino
winter l'inverno (m)
wiper blades le spazzole del tergicristallo
with con
withdraw (money) (verb) prelevare
withdrawal il prelievo
without senza
witness testimone (m/f)
woman la donna
work il lavoro
work (verb) lavorare
work (machine) funzionare
wrap (a gift) incartare
wrapping paper la carta a regalo
wrist il polso
wrist watch l'orologio da polso
wrong sbagliato/a

X, Y, Z

X-ray la radiografia
yacht lo yacht
year l'anno (m)
yellow giallo/a
yes sì
yesterday ieri
yoga lo yoga
you Lei; tu (singular); voi (plural)
zoo lo zoo

DICTIONARY ITALIAN–ENGLISH

The gender of Italian nouns is shown by the abbreviations (m)
for masculine and (f) for feminine. Plural nouns are followed
by the abbreviations (m pl) or (f pl). Adjectives vary according
to the gender and number of the word they describe. Here the
masculine singular form (usually "o") is shown, followed by the
alternative feminine ending (usually "a").

A

a at
abbastanza quite
abiti (m pl) clothes
abito (m) dress
abito da sera (m) evening
 dress
accamparsi to camp
accappatoio (m) bathrobe
accendere to light
accendino (m) lighter
acceso on (light)
accesso per i disabili (m)
 wheelchair access
acqua (f) water
adattatore (m) adapter
addebitare to charge
adulto (m) adult
aerobica (f) aerobics
aeroplano (m) airplane
aeroporto (m) airport
affittare to rent
affrettarsi to hurry
agenzia assicurativa (f)
 insurance company
agosto August
airbag (m) airbag
aiutare to help
albergo (m) hotel
album delle fotografie (m)
 photo album
alcuni/e some
aliscafo (m) hydrofoil
allarme antincendio (m)
 fire alarm
allergico/a allergic
allora then
altro/a other; **un altro/**
 un'altra another
ambasciata (f) embassy

ambulanza (f) ambulance
ambulatorio (m) doctor's
 office
americano/a (m/f)
 American
amico/a (m/f) friend
analisi del sangue (f pl)
 blood test
anche too (also)
ancora again
andare to go
andare a cavallo
 horseback riding
andare in discoteca to go
 clubbing
andare dritto to go straight
animale (m) domestico
 (m) pet
anno (m) year
antibiotici (m pl) antibiotics
antidolorifico (m) painkiller
anziano/a (m/f) senior
 citizen
ape (f) bee
aperto/a open
appartamento (m)
 apartment
appendiabiti (m) coat
 hanger
appuntamento (m)
 appointment
apribottiglie (m) bottle/can
 opener
aprile April
aprire to open
arancione orange (color)
area giochi (f) playground
aria condizionata (f)
 air conditioning
arrivare to arrive

arrivederci goodbye
arrivi (m pl) arrivals hall
arte (f) art
artrite (f) arthritis
ascensore (m) lift
asciugacapelli (m) hairdryer
asciugamano (m) towel
asciutto dry (day; clothes)
ascoltare to listen
asma (f) asthma
aspettare to wait
asse da stiro (f) ironing
  board
assegno (m) check
assicurazione (f) insurance
assicurazione sanitaria (f)
  health insurance
assistente di volo (f) flight
  attendant
assolato/a sunny
atrio (m) concourse
attraversamento pedonale
  (m) pedestrian crossing
attraverso through
attrezzatura (f) equipment
Australia (f) Australia
autobus (m) bus
automobile (f) car
autonoleggio (m) car rental
autopompa (f) fire engine
autostrada (f) highway
autunno (m) fall
aver bisogno to need
avere to have
avvocato (m) lawyer

B

bagagliaio (m) trunk (car);
  roofrack
bagaglio (m) luggage
bagaglio consentito (m)
  baggage allowance
bagaglio a mano (m) hand
  luggage
bagnato/a wet
bagnino (m) lifeguard
bagno (m) bath; bathroom;
  restroom
bagnoschiuma (m)
  bubblebath

balcone (m) balcony
ballare dancing
balsamo (m) conditioner
bambino/a (m/f) child
bambola (f) doll
banca (f) bank
bar (m) bar; café
barbecue (m) barbecue
barca (f) boat
barca a vela (f) sailboat
baseball (m) baseball
batteria (f) battery
bello/a beautiful; nice
benda (f) bandage
bene alright; well
benvenuto welcome
bere to drink
berlina (f) saloon car
bianco/a white
bibita (f) drink (noun)
bicchiere (m) glass
  (drinking)
bicicletta (f) bicycle,
  exercise bike
bidet (m) bidet
biglietteria automatica (f)
  automatic ticket machine
biglietto (m) ticket
biglietto di andata e ritorno
  (m) return ticket
biglietto d'entrata (m)
  entrance ticket
biglietto famiglia (m)
  family ticket
biglietto di sola andata (m)
  one-way ticket
bikini (m) bikini
binario (m) platform
blu blue
bocca (f) mouth
boccaglio (m) snorkel
bollitore (m) camping
  kettle; kettle
bordo: a bordo on board
borsa (f) bag; handbag
borsa per fotocamera (f)
  camera bag
bottiglia (f) bottle
boutique (f) boutique
bracciale (m) bracelet

braccio (m) arm
bretella (f) entrance/exit ramp
britannico/a British
bruciatura (f) burn
buonanotte good night
buonasera good evening
buongiorno hello
buono/a good
bussola (f) compass
busta (f) envelope
busto (m) bust

C

c'è there is
cabina (f) cabin
cabina del telefono (f)
    telephone booth
calcio (m) soccer (game)
caldo/a hot; warm
calmo/a calm
calzini (m pl) socks
calzoncini (m pl) shorts
cambiare to change
camera (f) room
camera a due letti (f) room
    with twin beds
camera doppia (f)
    double room
camera familiare (f)
    family room
camera singola (f)
    single room
cameriera (f) waitress
cameriere (m) waiter
camicia (f) shirt
camminare to walk
campeggio (m) campsite
camper (m) camper van
campo da golf (m)
    golf course
campo da tennis (m)
    tennis court
Canada (m) Canada
canale (m) channel (TV)
cancello (m) gate
cane (m) dog
canoa (f) canoe
cantante (m/f) singer
capelli (m pl) hair
capire to understand

cappello da sole (m)
    sun hat
cappotto (m) coat
capsula (f) capsule
carburante (m) gasoline
caro/a expensive
carrello (m) cart
carrozza ristorante (f)
    dining car
carta assegni (f)
    check card
carta di credito (f)
    credit card
carta d'identità (f) ID
carta d'imbarco (f)
    boarding pass
carta studenti (f)
    student card
carta telefonica (f)
    phone card
cartello (m) signpost
cartina (f) map; street map
cartolina (f) postcard
casa (f) house
cascata (f) waterfall
casco (m) cycling helmet
casinò (m) casino
cassa (f) checkout
    (supermarket)
casseruola (f) casserole dish
cassetta delle lettere (f)
    mailbox
castello (m) castle
catamarano (m) catamaran
cattedrale (f) cathedral
cattivo/a bad
cavatappi (m) corkscrew
caviglia (f) ankle
cavolo (m) cabbage
CD (m) CD
cellulare (m) cell phone
cena (f) dinner
cento hundred
centro commerciale (m)
    shopping mall
centro della città (m)
    town center
centro sportivo (m)
    sports center
cestino (m) basket

cestino da picnic (m) picnic basket

check-in (m) check in

chi? who?

chiamata a carico del destinatario (f) collect call

chiave (f) key

chiavetta USB (f) memory stick

chiesa (f) church

chilo (m) kilo

chilometro (m) kilometer

chiudere to close

chiudere a chiave to lock

chiuso/a closed

ci sono there are

ciao hello

ciascuno each

cibo (m) food

cin cin! cheers!

cinema (m) movie theater

cinquanta fifty

cinque five

cintura (f) belt

circa about

città (f) city; town

clacson (m) horn

cofano (m) hood (car)

colazione (f) breakfast

colino (m) colander

collana (f) necklace

collo (m) neck

collutorio (m) mouthwash

colpire to knock down

coltello (m) knife

come as; how; like

come? how

commissariato (m) police station

completo (m) suit

comprare to buy

comprendere to understand

compressa (f) pill; tablet

computer (m) computer

computer portatile (m) laptop

con with

concerto (m) concert

connettersi to log on

conoscere to know (people)

consigliare to recommend

consolato (m) consulate

console (m) consul

contento/a happy

contenuto (m) contents

conto (m) bill; check

conto bancario (m) bank account

controllo passaporti (m) passport control

coperta (f) blanket

coppia (f) pair

corda (f) string

cornice (f) photo frame

corpo (m) body

corriere (m) courier

corsia (f) ward

cosa? what?

così so

costa (f) coast

costume (m) swimsuit

crema (f) cream

crema per il corpo (f) body lotion

cruscotto (m) dashboard

cuccetta (f) sleeper berth

cucchiaino (m) teaspoon

cucchiaio (m) spoon

cucina (f) kitchen

cuscino (m) pillow

D

da by; from

danneggiato/a damaged

danza (f) ballet

dare to give

dare la precedenza to give way

data di scadenza (f) sell-by date

davanti front; in front of; opposite

delizioso/a delicious

denaro (m) cash; money

denti (m pl) teeth

dentifricio (m) toothpaste

dentista (m) dentist

denuncia (f) report (noun)

denunciare to report

deodorante (m) deodorant
depositare to deposit
deposito (m) deposit
deposito bagagli (m)
   left luggage
derubare to rob
destra: a destra right
   (direction)
detergente (m) detergent
detestare to hate
di of; than
diabetico/a diabetic
diarrea (f) diarrhea
dicembre December
dieci ten
diesel diesel
dietro a behind
digitare to key in
dipinto (m) painting
dire to say; to tell
direttore della banca (m)
   bank manager
disabile (m) disabled
   person
discese per i principianti
   (f pl) nursery slopes
disconnettersi to log out
disegno (m) drawing
distorsione (f) sprain
dito (m) finger
dito del piede (m) toe
divorziato/a divorced
doccia (f) shower
docciaschiuma (m) shower
   gel
documenti (m pl) papers
   (identity)
dodici twelve
dolce sweet; dessert
dolcificante (m) artificial
   sweetener
dolore (m) pain
domani tomorrow
domenica Sunday
donna (f) woman
dopo after
dottore (m) doctor
dove? where?
dovere to have to; must
   (verb)

due two
durante during

E

e and
ecografia (f) scan
edicola (f) newspaper kiosk
effetto indesiderato (m)
   side effect
effettuare un deposito
   to pay in
egli he
elettricista (m) electrician
elettricità (f) electricity
ella she
ellittica (f) cross trainer
e-mail (f) email
ematoma (m) bruise
entrata (f) entrance
epilettico/a epileptic
errore (m) mistake
eruzione (f) rash
esaminare to examine
esatto/a right (correct)
escoriazione (f) graze
escursionismo (m) hiking
essere to be
essere in debito to owe
esso/a it
est (m) east
estate (f) summer
estintore (m) fire
   extinguisher
euro (m) euro
extra extra

F

facchino (m) porter
famiglia (f) family
fare to do; to make
fare la spesa to go shopping
fare le valigie to pack
fare surf to surf
fari (m pl) headlights
farmacia (f) pharmacy
farmacista (m) pharmacist
faro (m) lighthouse
fasciatura (f) dressing
febbraio February
felice happy

fermare to stop
fermata dell'autobus (f) bus stop
ferramenta (f) hardware store
ferrovia (f) railroad
fetta (f) slice
fiammifero (m) match (light)
fidanzata (f) girlfriend
fidanzato (m) boyfriend
figlia (f) daughter
filtro solare (m) sunscreen
fine settimana (m) weekend
finire to finish
fino a until
firmare to sign
fiume (m) river
flash (m) flash gun
forbici (f pl) scissors
forbicine per le unghie (f pl) nail scissors
forchetta (f) fork
fornetto da campeggio (m) camping stove
forno (m) oven
forno a microonde (m) microwave
forse perhaps
forte strong
fotocamera (f) camera
fotocamera digitale (f) digital camera
fotografia (f) photograph
fotografia con il flash (f) flash photography
francobollo (m) stamp
frattura (f) fracture
frecce lampeggianti (f pl) hazard lights
freddo/a cold
fresco/a fresh
frigo portatile (m) cooler
frigorifero congelatore (m) fridge-freezer
fronte: di fronte a front; in front of; opposite
frullatore (m) blender
fruttivendolo (m) greengrocery

fumare to smoke
fumetto (m) comic
funivia (f) cable car
funzionare to work (machine)
fuori outside
furto (m) robbery

G

galleria (f) gallery (theater)
galleria d'arte (f) art gallery
gamba (f) leg
garage (m) garage
garanzia (f) guarantee
gas (m) gas
gastronomia (f) delicatessen
gemelli (m pl) cufflinks
generalmente usually
gennaio January
gente (f) people
ghiacciato/a icy
ghiaccio (m) ice
già already
giacca (f) jacket
giallo/a yellow
giardino (m) garden
ginocchio (m) knee
giocare to play (games)
giocattolo (m) toy
gioco (m) game
gioielleria (f) jewelry
gioielliere (m) jewelry store
giornale (m) newspaper
giorno (m) day
giorno festivo (m) public holiday
giostre (f pl) rides
giovedì Thursday
giro (m) tour
gita (f) trip
giubbotto di salvataggio (m) life jacket
giugno June
giusto/a right (correct)
gli the (m pl)
gola (f) throat
golf (m) golf
gomito (m) elbow
gomma a terra (f) flat tire

gomma da masticare (f)
chewing gum
gonna (f) skirt
gradi degrees
Gran Bretagna (f) Great
Britain
grande big; large
gratis free (no charge)
grattugia (f) grater
grave serious
grazie thank you
grembiule (m) apron
griglia (f) grill pan
gruppo (m) group
guancia (f) cheek
guanti da forno (m pl)
oven mitts
guanto da baseball (m)
baseball glove
guardare to look; to watch
guasto (m) breakdown
guida (f) guide; guidebook
guida audio (f) audio guide
guida turistica (f) tour guide
guidare to drive

H, I, J

hovercraft (m) hovercraft
idrante (m) hydrant
i the (m pl)
ieri yesterday
il the (m)
imbarcarsi to board
imbarcazione da diporto
(f) pleasure boat
impianto di riscaldamento
(m) heater
impianto stereo dell'
automobile (m) car stereo
in in
inalatore (m) inhaler
incartare to gift wrap
incidente (m) accident
incinta pregnant
incisione (f) engraving
indicatore di livello del
carburante (m) fuel gauge
indirizzo (m) address
indirizzo e-mail (m)
email address

indumenti impermeabili
(m pl) slickers
infermiera (f) nurse
infiammato/a sore
influenza (f) flu
infradito (f) flip-flop
inglese English
ingorgo (m) traffic jam
iniezione (f) injection
insalatiera (f) mixing bowl
interessante interesting
interessare to interest
Internet (m) internet
Internet cafè (m) internet
café
interprete (m/f) interpreter
intervento chirurgico (m)
operation (medical)
inventario (m) inventory
inverno (m) winter
inviare to send
io I
iPod (m) iPod
Italia (f) Italy
italiano/a Italian
jazz club (m) jazz club
jeans (m pl) jeans

L

la the (f)
là over there
ladro (m) thief
lago (m) lake
lampadina (f) light bulb
lasciare to check out (hotel);
to leave; to vacate
lassù up there
lavatrice (f) washing
machine
lavorare to work
lavoro (m) work; per lavoro
on business
le the (f pl)
leggere to read
leggero/a light
lei her (object)
lei she; Lei you
lente (f) lens
lento/a slow
lettino (m) crib

lettino sdraio (m) lounge chair
letto (m) bed
letto matrimoniale (m) double bed
lettore CD (m) CD player
lettore DVD (m) DVD player
leva del cambio (f) gear shift
libero/a free (not occupied)
libreria (f) book store
libretto degli assegni (m) checkbook
libro (m) book
limite di velocità (m) speed limit
linea (f) line
lista (f) list
lo the (m)
locale local
lontano far
loro their; they
lozione solare (f) suntan lotion
lucchetto (m) lock
luce (f) light (noun)
lucido gloss
luglio July
lui he; him
luna park (m) fairground
lunedì Monday
lungo/a long
luogo (m) place

M

macchina (f) car; machine
macelleria (f) butcher's
madre (f) mother
maggio May
maglio (m) mallet
maglione (m) sweater
mai never
mal di denti (m) toothache
mal di stomaco stomach ache
mal di testa (m) headache
malato/a ill
malattia (f) illness
mandare to send
mangiare to eat

maniglia (f) handle
mano (f) hand
manoscritto (m) manuscript
mappa (f) map; street map
mare (m) sea
marito (m) husband
marmitta (f) exhaust (car)
martedì Tuesday
mascella (f) jaw
materasso (m) mattress
matita (f) pencil
mattino (m) morning
mazza (f) golf club
meccanico (m) mechanic
medicina (f) medicine
medusa (f) jellyfish
meno less
mento (m) chin
menù (m) menu
mercato (m) market
mercoledì Wednesday
mese (m) month
messaggio (m) message
metà half
metropolitana (f) subway
mettere to put
mezzanotte midnight
mezzo medium; middle; half
mezzogiorno noon
mia/mie my (f/f pl))
mini bar (m) mini bar
minuto (m) minute
mio/miei my (m/m pl))
misto/a mixed
modulo (m) form
moglie (f) wife
molti/e many
moltissimo very much
molto much; very
montagna (f) mountain
monumento (m) monument
moto d'acqua (m) jet ski
motocicletta (f) motorcycle
motore (m) engine
mountain bike (f) mountain bike
mouse (m) mouse (computer)

multa (f) fine (legal)
municipio (m) town hall
museo (m) museum
musica (f) music
musicista (m) musician

N

naso (m) nose
nausea (f) nausea
nebbioso/a misty
negozio (m) store
negozio di arredamento
  (m) furniture store
negozio di articoli da
  regalo (m) gift shop
negozio di dischi record
  store
negozio duty-free (m)
  duty-free shop
neo (m) mole (medical)
nero/a black
niente anything; nothing
nightclub (m) nightclub
no no
noi us; we
noleggiare to rent; to hire
nome (m) name
non not
nord (m) north
nostro/nostri/nostra/
  nostre our
notte (f) night
nove nine
novembre November
numero (m) number
numero di conto (m)
  account number
numero di targa (m)
  registration number
numero di telefono (m)
  contact number
nuoto (m) swimming
nuovo/a new
nuvoloso/a cloudy

O

o or
occhiali (m pl) glasses
occhiali da sole (m pl)
  sunglasses

occhialini (m pl) goggles
occhio (m) eye
odiare to hate
oggetti di valore (m pl)
  valuables
oggi today
ogni each (every)
olio (m) oil
ombrello (m) umbrella
ombrellone da spiaggia
  (m) beach umbrella
online online
opaco/a matte
opera (f) opera
ora (f) hour
orario (m) timetable
orario delle visite (m)
  visiting hours
orario di apertura (m)
  opening hours
ordinare to order
ordine (m) order
orecchio (m) ear
ormeggio (m) mooring
orologio da polso (m)
  wrist watch
orribile awful
ospedale (m) hospital
ospite (f/m) guest
otto eight
ottobre October
ovest (m) west

P

pacchetto (m) pack
padella (f) frying pan
padre (m) father
paese (m) country; village
pagare to pay
pagare in contanti
  to pay cash
palestra (f) gym
paletta (f) dust pan
palla (f) ball
palla da golf (f) golf ball
palla da tennis (f)
  tennis ball
pallone (m) soccer (ball)
pallone da spiaggia (m)
  beach ball

panetteria (f) bakery
panne: in panne broken (in car)
parabrezza (m) windshield
paraurti (m) bumper
parcheggiare to park
parcheggio (m) parking
parcheggio per disabili (m) disabled parking
parchimetro (m) parking meter
parco (m) park
parco a tema (m) theme park
parco safari (m) safari park
parlare to speak
parte posteriore (f) back (not front of)
partenze (f pl) departures
partire to depart; to leave
partita (f) match (sport)
pass per lo ski-lift (m) lift pass
passaporto (m) passport
passeggero (m) passenger
passeggiata (f) walk
pasto a bordo (m) in-flight meal
patente di guida (f) driver's license
patologia cardiaca (f) heart condition
pattumiera (f) garbage can
pedaggio (m) toll
pelle (f) skin
peluche (m) stuffed animal
penna (f) pen
pensare to think
pensione: in pensione retired
pentola (f) saucepan
per for
per favore please
perché? why?
perdere to lose
perdita (f) leak
persone (f pl) people
pesce (m) fish
pescivendolo (m) fish seller
pezzo (m) piece

piacere to like
piacevole nice
pianista (m) pianist
piattino (m) saucer; side plate
piatto (m) dish; plate
piazza (f) square (in town)
picchetto (m) tent peg
piccolo/a small; little
picnic (m) picnic
piede (m) foot
pieno/a full
pilates pilates
pilota (m) pilot
PIN (m) PIN number
pinne (f pl) flippers
piove to rain
piscina (f) swimming pool
più more
pneumatico (m) tire
poco little
poggiatesta (m) head rest
poi then
polizia (f) police
poliziotta (f) policewoman
poliziotto (m) policeman
polizza (f) policy
polizza assicurativa (f) insurance policy
pollice (m) thumb
polso (m) wrist
pomata (f) ointment
pomeriggio (m) afternoon
pompa (f) pump
pompiere (m) firefighter
porta (f) door
portafoglio (m) wallet
portamonete (m) change purse
portare to carry; da portar via carry out
portellone (m) hatchback
porticciolo (m) marina
porto (m) harbor
posate (f pl) cutlery
possibile possible
posta (f) post
posta aerea (f) airmail
posteggio dei taxi (m) taxi stand

postino (m) postman
posto (m) place; seat
posto vicino al corridoio
(m) aisle seat
posto vicino al finestrino
(m) window seat
potere can (verb)
pranzo (m) lunch
preferito/a favorite
prelevare to withdraw
(money)
prelievo (m) withdrawal
prendere to take
prenotare to book; reserve
prenotazione (f) reservation
pressione arteriosa elevata
(f) high blood pressure
pressione degli pneumatici
(f) tire pressure
presto early; soon
prezzo (m) price
prima di before
primavera (f) spring
primo/a first
principiante (m/f) beginner
prolunga (f) extension cord
pronto/a ready
Pronto Soccorso (m)
accident and emergency
prossimo/a next
provare to try
pulito/a clean

Q

qualche volta sometimes
qualcosa anything
qualcosa something
qualcuno/a somebody
quale? which?
quando? when?
quanti/e? how many?
quanto? how much?
quaranta forty
quasi almost
quattordici fourteen
quattro four
quello/a that
questo/a this
qui here
quindici fifteen

R

racchetta da tennis (f)
tennis racket
racchette da sci (f pl)
ski poles
radiatore (m) radiator
radio (f) radio
radiografia (f) X-ray
raffreddore (m) cold
(illness)
raffreddore da fieno (m)
hay fever
ragazzo/a (m/f) boy/girl
rampa per i disabili (f)
wheelchair ramp
rapido/a quick
rasoio (m) razor
rasoio elettrico (m)
electric razor
reato (m) crime
reclamare to complain
regalo (m) gift; present
rene (m) kidney (medical)
reparto di terapia intensiva
(m) intensive care unit
repellente per gli insetti
(m) insect repellent
retro (m) back (not front of)
rianimazione (f)
resuscitation
riavviare to reboot
ricetta medica (f)
prescription
ricevuta (f) bill; receipt
ricevuta dei bagagli (f)
baggage claim check
riduzione (f) reduction
riempire to fill
rimorchiare to tow
riparare to fix; repair
riparazione (f) repair
riscaldamento (m) heating
riscaldamento centralizzato
(m) central heating
riscuotere to cash
riservare to reserve
ristorante (m) restaurant
ritardo: in ritardo late
ritiro bagagli (m)
baggage claim

rivelatore di fumo (m) smoke alarm
rivista (f) magazine
rosa pink
rosso/a red
rotatoria (f) traffic circle
rotondo/a round
rotto/a broken
rubato/a stolen
rubinetto di arresto (m) water valve
rullino (m) roll (of film)
ruota (f) tire; wheel
ruota di scorta (f) spare tire
rusta (f) whisk

S

sabato Saturday
sabbia (f) sand
sacca da viaggio (f) carryall
sacco a pelo (m) sleeping bag
sala d'attesa (f) waiting room
salute (f) health
salvagente (m) lifebuoy
sandali (m pl) sandals
sangue dal naso (m) nosebleed
sapere to know (a fact)
sapone (m) soap
sarto (m) tailor
sbagliato/a wrong
sbucciatore (m) peeler
scale (f pl) stairs
scarpa (f) shoe
scarpe da ginnastica (f pl) sneakers
scarpone (m) boot
scarponi (m pl) hiking boots
scarponi da sci (m pl) ski boots
scatola (f) box
scatola dei fusibili (f) fuse box
scatoletta (f) can (noun)
scendere to get off
scheda di memoria (f) memory card

scheggia (f) splinter
schiena (f) back (body)
schiuma da barba (f) shaving foam
sci (m pl) skis
sci (m) skiing
sci d'acqua (m) water-skiing
scodella (f) bowl
scompartimento (m) compartiment
scopa (f) brush (cleaning)
scotch (m) adhesive tape
scottatura solare (f) sunburn
scrivania (f) desk
scusi sorry
secchio (m) bucket
secco dry (wine)
secondo/a second
sedia a rotelle (f) wheelchair
sedia a sdraio (f) deck chair
seggiolino (m) child seat
seggiolone (m) high chair
seggiovia (f) chair lift
segnali stradali (m pl) road signs
sei six
semaforo (m) traffic lights
sentire to hear
senza without
senza piombo unleaded
separatamente separately
sera (f) evening
serpente (m) snake
servire to serve
servizi di emergenza (m pl) emergency services
servizio di babysitting (m) babysitting
servizio espresso (m) express service
sette seven
settembre September
settimana (f) week
shampoo (m) shampoo
sì yes
sicuro/a safe
sigaretta (f) cigarette
sinistra left

sito Web (m) website

soggiorno (m) stay

solamente only

soldi (m pl) money

sole (m) Sun

solito/a usual

solo/a alone

sopra over

sotto below; beneath

souvenir (m) souvenir

spalla (f) shoulder

spatola (f) spatula

spazzolino da denti (m)
toothbrush

specialità (f) specialty

spedire la posta to mail

spegnere to turn off

spento/a off

spesso often

spiaggia (f) beach

spina (f) plug

spogliatoio (m) changing
room

sport (m) sport

sportello bancomat (m)
cash machine

sposato/a married

spray (m) spray

spuntino (m) snack

stagione (f) season

stampa (f) print (photo)

stampare to print

stanza libera (f) vacancy
(room)

starnutire to sneeze

stasera tonight

Stati Uniti (m pl) United
States

statua (f) statue

stazione (f) railroad station

stazione degli autobus (f)
bus station

stazione di servizio (f) gas
station

stecca (f) splint

step machine (f)
step machine

sterlina (f) British pound

stesso/a same

stitichezza (f) constipation

stivale (m) boot

stomaco (m) stomach

strada (f) road; street; way

stretto tight

studente/studentessa
(m/f) student

su on; over; up

succedere to happen

sud (m) south

suo/sua/sue his; her; your

supermercato (m)
supermarket

supposte (f pl)
suppositories

surfista (m/f) windsurfer

svaligiare to burgle

sveglia telefonica (f)
wake-up call

sviluppare to develop (film)

T

tabaccaio (m) tobacco shop

tabacco (m) tobacco

tachimetro (m)
speedometer

taglia (f) size

tagliaunghie (m) nail
clippers

tagliere (m) cutting board

taglio (m) cut

tallone (m) heel

tardi late

tasso di cambio (m)
exchange rate

tastiera (f) keyboard

tavola da surf (f) surfboard

tavoletta (f) float

tavolo (m) table

taxi (m) taxi

tazza (f) cup

teatro (m) theater

teatro dell'opera (m)
opera house

teglia da forno (f)
cookie sheet

telecomando (m)
remote control

telefonare to telephone

telefonata (f) phone call

telefono (m) telephone

televisore (m) television
televisore a schermo
  panoramico (m)
  widescreen TV
telo da spiaggia (m)
  beach towel
temperatura (f) temperature
tempestoso/a stormy
tempo time
tempo (m) weather
tenda (f) tent
tenda veneziana (f)
  Venetian blind
tennis (m) tennis
tergicristallo (m) windshield
  wiper
terminal (m) terminal
termostato (m) thermostat
testa (f) head
testimone (m/f) witness
thermos (m) vacuum flask
torace (m) chest
torcia (f) flashlight
tosse (f) cough
tovagliolo (m) napkin
traghetto (m) ferry
travellers cheque (m)
  traveler's check
tre three
treno (m) train
trenta thirty
troppo too
trovare to find
T-shirt (f) T-shirt
tu you
turista (m/f) tourist
tutto/i all
TV satellitare (f) satelliteTV

U, V, Y, Z

ufficio del turismo (m)
  tourist information office
ufficio oggetti smarriti (m)
  lost property
ufficio postale (m) post
  office
ultimo/a last
umido/a humid
undici eleven
unghia (f) nail

uno/a one
uomo (m) man
urgente urgent
usare to use
uscita (f) exit
uscita d'imbarco (f)
  boarding gate
utile useful
vacanza (f) vacation
valigetta (f) briefcase
valigia (f) suitcase
valore (m) value
vedere to see
vegetariano/a vegetarian
vela (f) sailing
veloce fast; quick
vendere to sell
venerdì Friday
venire to come
venti twenty
ventilatore (m) fan
ventoso/a windy
veramente really
verde green
vespa (f) wasp
vetro (m) glass
via (f) street; way
viaggio (m) travel
vicino close (near)
vicino a beside; by; next to
videogioco (m) video game
vidimare to validate
vigneto (m) vineyard
villaggio (m) village
vino (m) wine
violenza carnale (f) rape
visita guidata (f) guided tour
visitatore (m) visitor
viso (m) face
vista (f) view
visto (m) visa
voi you (pl)
volante (f) police car
volere to want
volo (m) flight
yacht (m) yacht
yoga (m) yoga
zaino (m) backpack
zoo (m) zoo

NUMBERS

1 uno *oonoh*	9 nove *novay*	17 diciasette *deechasettay*	70 settanta *settantah*
2 due *dooeh*	10 dieci *deeaychee*	18 diciotto *deechottoh*	80 ottanta *ottantah*
3 tre *tray*	11 undici *oondeechee*	19 diciannove *deechano-vay*	90 novanta *novantah*
4 quattro *kwattroh*	12 dodici *dodeechee*	20 venti *ventee*	100 cento *chentoh*
5 cinque *cheenkway*	13 tredici *traydeechee*	30 trenta *trentah*	1,000 mille *meelay*
6 sei *say*	14 quattordici *kwattor-deechee*	40 quaranta *kwarantah*	10,000 diecimila *deeaychee-meelah*
7 sette *settay*	15 quindici *kweend-eechee*	50 cinquanta *cheenkwan-tah*	1,000,000 un milione *oon meelyo-nay*
8 otto *ottoh*	16 sedici *sedeechee*	60 sessanta *sessantah*	

ORDINAL NUMBERS

first primo *preemoh*	fourth quarto *kwartoh*	seventh settimo *setteemoh*	tenth decimo *decheemoh*
second secondo *sekondoh*	fifth quinto *kweentoh*	eighth ottavo *otahvoh*	twentieth ventesimo *ventezee-moh*
third terzo *tertsoh*	sixth sesto *sestoh*	ninth nono *nonoh*	

PICTURE CREDITS

Key: a (above); b (below/bottom); c (centre); l (left);
r (right); t (top)

Alamy Images: Alvey & Towers Picture Library p111 cb;
PhotoSpin, Inc p36 crb; Tetra Images p 18; **Courtesy of
Renault:** p24–25 t; **Getty Images:** Reggie Casagrande p146;
PunchStock: Moodboard p6
All other images © Dorling Kindersley